YoungWriters 2005 POE

PLAYGROU

Let your creativity flow...

ode
limerick haiku
rhyme
ball

West Yorkshire
Edited by Sarah Marshall

 Young**Writers**

First published in Great Britain in 2005 by:
Young Writers
Remus House
Coltsfoot Drive
Peterborough
PE2 9JX
Telephone: 01733 890066
Website: www.youngwriters.co.uk

SB ISBN 1 84602 133 2

Foreword

Young Writers was established in 1991 and has been passionately devoted to the promotion of reading and writing in children and young adults ever since. The quest continues today. Young Writers remains as committed to the fostering of burgeoning poetic and literary talent as ever.

This year's Young Writers competition has proven as vibrant and dynamic as ever and we are delighted to present a showcase of the best poetry from across the UK. Each poem has been carefully selected from a wealth of *Playground Poets* entries before ultimately being published in this, our thirteenth primary school poetry series.

Once again, we have been supremely impressed by the overall high quality of the entries we have received. The imagination, energy and creativity which has gone into each young writer's entry made choosing the best poems a challenging and often difficult but ultimately hugely rewarding task - the general high standard of the work submitted amply vindicating this opportunity to bring their poetry to a larger appreciative audience.

We sincerely hope you are pleased with our final selection and that you will enjoy *Playground Poets West Yorkshire* for many years to come.

Contents

Lauren Wilson (9)   15
Kerry Waite (10)   15
Zoë Meek (10)   16
Ashleigh Davies (8)   16
Ruth Belchetz (9)   17
Jamie Heeley (9)   17
Eliot Dixon (9)   18
Callum Barnham & Tom Boyes-Park (9)   18
Sophie Mirczuk (9)   19
Maggie Cunningham (8)   19
Emily Anne Wood (11)   19
Rhonwen Powell (8)   20
Alice Clews (9)   20
Oliver Ledingham Smith (11)   21
Ben Horner (10)   21
Aileen Maria Duffy (8)   22
Hannah Priestley (9)   22
Jordan Brown (9)   23
Cath Noble (9)   23
Jamie Edward Lock (9)   24
Elliot Clayton (9)   24
Charlotte I'Anson (9)   24
Harrison Grange (8)   25
Sophie Young (7)   25
Richard Gorvin (10)   26
Sarah Whitla (11)   26
Abie Roberts (9)   26
Chris Lyons (11)   27
Graeme Duffy (7)   27
George Grange (10)   27
Ross Goddard (9)   28
Harry Akitt (7)   28
Robbie Eardley (8)   29

Gawthorpe JI & N School

Ellie May Clark (7)   29
Emily Layton (10)   30
Alice Scales (10)   30
Brogan Gale (10)   31
Chloé Jaye Ottewell (10)   31
Jordan Crosland (10)   32

Amy Watson (8) 32
Megan Crabtree (11) 33
Courtnie Calcutt (11) 33
Joanne Rourke (10) 34
Nathan Sorby (11) 35
Christopher Skevington (11) 36
Christian Reddyhoff (10) 36
Daniel Rooney (11) 37
Dale Treloar (11) 37
Robert Wilson (11) 38
Matthew Kitchen (9) 38
Laura-Molly Walker (11) 39
Oliver Brown (8) 39
Natalie Summerscales (9) 40
Chloe Dewhirst (10) 41
Eleanor Burkinshaw (9) 42
Alexander Green (10) 42
Alice Ramsden (10) 43
Jonathon Wilson (9) 43
Kimberley Harris (10) 44
Liam Ward (10) 45
Lauren Smith (10) 46
Zoe Sheard (8) 46
Joel Driver (10) 47
Jack Hayman (8) 47
Damien Cresswell (10) 48
Laura Gomersall (9) 49
Charlotte Williamson (9) 50
Catherine Morton (9) 51
Cameron Burns (9) 52
Andrew Rourke (8) 52
Emma Dixon (9) 53
James Heighton (9) 53

Manston Primary School

Elisha Merriman (11) 54
Shelby Douglas (11) 55
Beth Matthews (11) 56
James Duckworth (10) 56
Annabel Riley (10) 57
Andrew Horry (10) 57

James Padmore (11)	58
Georgina Price (11)	58
Lynsey Beaumont (11)	59
Alex Proctor (11)	59
Joseph Cooney (11)	60
Holly Anna Robinson (11)	60
Chelsea Lee Holmes (10)	61
Aimee L Routledge (10)	61
Jade Louise Towers (11)	62
Joe Bilbey (11)	62
Rebecca Croft (11)	63
Liam Berry (11)	63
Victoria Scholes (11)	64
Jake Bleasby (10)	64

Manston St James CE Primary School

Jack Young (9)	65
Natalie Wainman (8)	65
Laura Weed (9)	66
Abigail Moss (7)	66
Tomas Spink (9)	67
Jack McMaster (8)	67
Natasha Round (8)	68
Alycia Rose Milner (10)	68
Hayden Pride (9)	69
James Sanderson (8)	69
Jack Nelmes (9)	70
Thomas Fisher (8)	70
Natalie Austin (8)	70
Seb Marsh (9)	71
Abigail Heraty (9)	71
Jason Moore (9)	72
Amelia Scott (7)	72
Danielle Manning (8)	73
Harriet Laverick (9)	73
Molly Jones (9)	74
Lauren Huddlestone (8)	74
Harriet Darcy (9)	75
Alexander Crosbie-Wright (8)	75
Dominic Evans (8)	76
Andrew Battye (11)	76

Kia Clinton-Muncey (8)	77
Laura Dixon (11)	77
Luke Cheetham (9)	78
Ashley Walls (11)	78
Kristan-lewis Bratton (9)	79
Ashley Hullock (11)	79
Dean Bland (9)	80
Charles Dunkley (11)	80
Shaun Binns (9)	81
Azrael Bell (9)	81
Jack Wildsmith (10)	82
Laura Place (10)	82
Sophie Jagger (10)	83
Alfie Leeds (11)	83
Jenny Tootell (10)	84
Rosie Allen (10)	84
Rachel Clark (11)	84
Rebecca Gibbs (11)	85
Emma Sutcliffe (10)	85
Dylan Parr (10)	85
Emma Gelley (11)	86
Adam Kerrigan (11)	86
Jennifer Dunwell (10)	87
Jennifer Roberts (11)	87
Chelsea Shepherd (11)	88
Jessica Nolan (11)	88
Alice Lane (11)	89
Thomas Appleyard (10)	89
Elliot Walls (11)	90
Leigh Towse (11)	90
Amy Wood (10)	91
Mathew Kerry (10)	91
Lucy Packman (11)	91
Megan Boldison (11)	92
Lauren Heraty (11)	92

Moorfield School

Emily Thomson (10)	92
Emma Goodwin-Jones (10)	93
Lauren Richardson (11)	93
Emily Layton (11)	93

Georgie Henley (9)	94
Bethan Daykin (9)	95
Emily Wood (8)	95
Rosie Phillip (7)	96
Emma Tankard (8)	96
Enya-Medi Wentling (7)	97
Laura Layton (8)	97
Ellie-Mai Driver (6)	98
Abigail Stott (7)	98
Stephanie Ford (10)	99
Millie Clapham (6)	99
Amy Bolser (10)	100
Sophie Stone (10)	100
Emma Dracup (9)	101
Martha Crossley (10)	101
Bryony Skinn (9)	102
Emma Tapper (9)	102

North Featherstone J&I School

John Best (8)	103
Victoria Rennison (9)	103
Joe Roberts (9)	104
Ethan Vickers (9)	104
Katie Morgan (8)	105
Meg Nowell (7)	105
Abigail Ziemniak (9)	106
Ella Gibbs (8)	106
Melissa Guest (9)	107
Scott Lapish (8)	107
Adam Nix (9)	108
Katie Crawshaw (9)	108
Sarah Pashley (9)	109
Samantha Still (9)	109

Our Lady's Primary School

Grace Somerville (10)	109
Jessica Beaumont (8)	110
Natasha Griffiths (10)	110
Elliott Wilkes (9)	111
Brad Cascarino (10)	111
Bobby Jones (8)	112

Katie-Louise Smith (10)   112
Marco Longoni (10)   112
Thomas Hind (9)   113
Tyler Vayro   113
Matthew Wild (9)   113
Lauren Clarke (9)   114
Jonty Lendill (9)   114
Leah Gatenby (10)   114
Matthew Gavaghan (9)   115
Holly Kneale McKeon (10)   115
Julianne Ruocco (10)   115
James Clark Dixon (9)   116
Courtney Gunby (9)   116
Liam Maddock (10)   116
Josh Hooks (8)   117
Hayley Webster (9)   117
Ben O'Connell (8)   117
Jason Stevenson (9)   118
Georgia Wade (8)   118
Nathan Sykes (8)   119
Ryan Rowlands (9)   119
Aaron Roberts (8)   120
Joshua Padmore (8)   120
Joshua Reed (8)   121
Joe Harper (8)   121
Daniel Phillips (9)   121

Richmond House School

Benjamin Kemp (7)   122
Francesca Broadbridge-Kirbitson (7)   122
Sam Sheehy (7)   123
Lucas Smedley (7)   123
Charlotte Denison (10)   124
Harrison Brown Raw (7)   124
Henry Cranston (10)   125
Alex Barnett (7)   125
Ashley Hemingway (11)   126
Edward West (7)   126
Eleanor Heffron (10)   127
Paul Millner (7)   127
Hannah Donkin (10)   128

Robin Butler (7) — 128
Joe Whitehurst (11) — 129
Jonathan Webster (7) — 129
William Harrison (10) — 130
Keyanur Bennett (10) — 130
Molly Smith (9) — 131
Josef Baczkowski (9) — 131
Holly Stenton (10) — 132
Jayarjun Deu (9) — 132
Jessica Armstrong (8) — 133
Aoife Jackson (7) — 133
James Bastin (7) — 134
Amelia Mary Crump (7) — 134
Sam Kavanagh (7) — 135
Nayab Chaudhry (10) — 135
Fred Kamstra (11) — 136
Edward Sargeant (7) — 136
James Wilson (11) — 137
Chantelle Joslin (10) — 137
Sian Gatenby (10) — 138
Gosha Smith (7) — 138
Anthony West (10) — 139
Jennie Stubbs (10) — 139
Malkit Sihra (10) — 140
William Peckham (9) — 140
Molly Hayward (10) — 141
Sebby May (10) — 141
Simran Bhullar (9) — 142
Hannah Gatenby (8) — 142
Charlotte Barraclough (11) — 143
James Richert (9) — 143
Hugo Calder (8) — 144
Zac Campsall-Bhatti (10) — 144
Joe Kamstra (9) — 145
Davy Ker (9) — 146
Lottie McMahon (9) — 147
Joshua Frazer (9) — 147
Matthew Chan (10) — 148
Jac Moore (11) — 148
Marcus Gay (9) — 149
Luke Richert (9) — 149
Charlotte Martin (10) — 150

Rory Denison (8)   171
Holly Lenahan (7)   172
Matthew Harris (9)   172
William Masterton (8)   173

Roberttown J&I School

Sam Crossley (10)   173
Kellie-Jo Jeffery (10)   174
Sam Bull (11)   174
Kirsty Crowther (10)   175
Laylaa Whittaker (10)   175
Joshua Glassett (10)   176
Olivia Ledgard (11)   176
Brittany Stead (8)   177
Amy Peacock (10)   177
Kirsty Gee & Rachel Secker (10)   178
Ellen Bellfield (10)   178
Sam Gaunt (7)   179
Georgina Barry (10)   179
Lydia Glassett (8)   180
Hamza Nawaz (9)   180
Connor Balach (10)   181
Callum McDermott (8)   181
Emily Tench (8)   182
James Ives (7)   182
Bethany Stead (10)   183
James Thomas (8)   183
Ellena Roberts (7)   184
Helen Edmond (9)   184
Amber Shaw (8)   185
Sara Jayne Pollard (11)   185
Chelsea Mitchell (10)   186
Rachel Glaves (7)   187
Joseph Allatt (8)   187
Charlotte Glaves (9)   188
Callum Pickles (8)   188
Jack Smith (7)   189
Jennifer Hurst (8)   189
Ellie Walker (8)   190
Robin Eloise Barraclough (7)   190
Matthew Brook (11)   190

Alicia Kemp (7)   191
Daniel Mott (10)   191
Daniel Collins (7)   192
James Ross & Alastair McDonald (10)   192
Robert Ives & David Hall (11)   192

St Chad's CE Primary School, Brighouse

Amelia Carter (10)   193
Benedict Barron (10)   193
Emma Baldwin (10)   194
Ryan Sharp (9)   194
George Pearson (9)   195
Conor Durkin (9)   195
Victoria Pearson (9)   196
Daniel Burnside (9)   196
Bethany Dimmock (10)   197
Victoria Wetton (10)   197
Jessica Hagain (9)   198
Andrew Maycock (10)   198
Peter Walker (10)   199
Lewis Reid (9)   199
Jamie Shackleton (9)   200
Bradley Seymour (9)   200
Nicole Riach (10)   201
Nathaniel Leah (9)   201
Beth Adamson (9)   202
Luke Baranyai (9)   202
Kirsty Monday (10)   203

St Helen's CE Aided J&I School, Pontefract

Connor Trevelyan & Adam Cockayne (8)   203
Joshua Conway, Nathan Cargill, Connor Trevelyan, Jonathan
    Deaville, Kieran Olbison, Curtis Petch & Jay Cook   204
Aidan Garrett & Jonathan Deaville (7)   204
Year 3 (8)   204
Year 3 (8)   205
Jack Hiley, Liam Goodlad, Shauna Mee, Katy Skidmore, Olivia
    Dickens & Joshua Ryan (8)   205

St John's CE (A) J&I School, Golcar

Simon Bottomley (9)	205
Nat Gregory (9)	206
Megan Woods (10)	207
Alex Jones (9)	207
Jack Midwood (9)	208
Eleanor Smith (9)	208
Sarah Nixon (10)	209
Grace Young-Roberts (9)	209
Melissa Whitwam (10)	210
Connor Fawcett (9)	210
Annie Shaw (10)	211
Jack Lockwood (9)	211
Charlotte Fox (9)	212
Reece Sykes (10)	212
Joshua Woods (9)	213
Nathan Firth (9)	213
Molly Ashmore (10)	214
Laura Mallalieu (9)	214
Haydn Todd (10)	215
Callum Peel (9)	215
Limara Gay (10)	216
Harry Hutchinson (9)	216
Callum Mair (10)	217
Leigh-Amy Ruff (10)	217
Darcy Edgar (9)	218
Katie O'Brien (9)	218
Victoria Atkinson (10)	218
Chelsea Redshaw (9)	219

St Patrick's Primary School, Birstall

Matthew Bramham (8)	219
Fay Brown (8)	219
Mia Green (7)	220
Connor Butterfield (7)	220
Bradley Flavell (8)	221
Patrick Flowers (7)	221
Joseph Foster (7)	221
Holly Speight (8)	222
Olivia Hilton (8)	222
Kieran Goodman (8)	222

George O'Hara (7)	223
Nathan Jones (7)	223
Siobhan Orange (7)	223
Laura Russell (7)	224
Nadiah Kazzan (8)	224
Chantel Morris (8)	224
Conor Harrington (7)	225
Max Senior (7)	225
Hannah Senior (7)	225
Chloe Barrett (7)	226
Patrick Sykes (8)	226
Tom Bottomley (7)	226
Alex Burnett (8)	226

Sutton-In-Craven CP School

Sinead White (9)	227
Joshua Wood (9)	227
Tanya Hunter (11)	228
Becky Simpson (10)	228
Kayleigh Davies (11)	229
Leah Thompson (9)	229
Braidi Woods (10)	229

Wakefield Tutorial School

Jessica Clegg (10)	230
Felicia Doubell (11)	231
Jacob Atkinson (9)	232
Imogen Wade (9)	233
Holly Taylor-Whitehead (9)	233
Holly Latham (9)	234
Joseph Elliott (9)	235
James Rathmell (8)	236
Anna Sheldon (9)	237
George Judd (8)	237
Amy Cassar (8)	238

Westville House School

Charlotte Alton (9)	239
Ellen Dewhurst (8)	239
Kodie Brook (8)	240

The Poems

I See A Little Dog

I see a little dog
I see a little dog, he plays all day
I see a little dog, he runs very fast when he gets my toys
I see a little dog, a little white dog
I see a little dog, he is quite chubby, but when he has a bath he is fine
I see a little dog, he is soft like a coat
I see a little dog, with a loud bark
I see a little dog, he goes under the sofa, he scratches
                                   and makes a guinea pig noise
I see a little dog, he bites my shoes.

Nicola Hudson (8)

Sadness

Sadness is blue, like tears falling from your eyes.
Sadness sounds like a girl crying in the house on the red couch.
Sadness tastes like freezing cold water evaporating from your hands.
Sadness smells like a blue flower full of clear tears dropping
                                         from the petals.

Jordan Mills (9)
Ackworth Howard CE J&I School

Love

Love is a great big cuddle.
Love is the colour pink.
Love tastes like sweet smoothies, ready to drink, yum-yum in my tum.
Love smells like sweet and sour sauce.
Love looks like a small vase of flowers.

Emma Clowes (8)
Ackworth Howard CE J&I School

Love

Love is the colour of a sunrise
that reflects off a pond.
When you see each other
your heart starts beating and sometimes you freeze.
If you are hurt, you look at each other
and the pain goes away.
A tear runs down your face.

Danielle Watkiss-Findley (8)
Ackworth Howard CE J&I School

Fear

Fear is white like a pale ghost.
It sounds like feet stomping towards you.
Fear tastes like weak coffee, no flavour at all.
It smells like old rotting mummies from Egypt.
Fear looks like a lightning bolt ready to strike at any time.
It feels like a holly leaf, very spiky.
Fear reminds me of falling out with my friends.

Connor Joshua Spencer (9)
Ackworth Howard CE J&I School

Fun

Fun is playing with my best friend's cat.
Fun is a ball and baseball bat,
Playing with my mum and my grandma's cat.
Fun is skipping in the playground.
Fun is going to the cricket ground,
Sat with all the other people making lots of sounds.
Fun is having three best friends.
Fun with my friends never ends.

Danielle Cookson (9)
Ackworth Howard CE J&I School

Pets

Some pets are lovely, some are nasty,
Some live in square homes, some live in round ones,
Like the active hamster running round and round its house,
Some live way up high, high in the sky, like a bird that likes to fly,
Some pets like to fight, some pets like to play all day,
Some live in water and swim round and round, up and down,
                                    watching the world go by,
Lots of different people have lots of different pets,
In lots of different homes, so all you people out there,
Look after your pets well.

Sophie Fox (9)
Ackworth Howard CE J&I School

Love

Love is the colour of a sweet gentle pink.
Love makes the sound of a cooing baby.
Love tastes like melted chocolate, gooey, runny and sweet.
Love smells like the perfume of a rose
And looks like a baby's smile.
It feels like fairies' wings, all glittery, soft and silky.
Last of all, it reminds me of my sister's smiley face.

Rachel Burgess (9)
Ackworth Howard CE J&I School

Dragons

D aring dragons strong and fierce
R oar so big, so powerful
A ttacking the enemy
G reen skin with slimy teeth
O n coming more dragons
N othing with stop them
S piky backs that shoot up in the air to defend themselves.

Lydia Bagg (8)
Ackworth Howard CE J&I School

The Monster From Mars

I can see a monster from Mars
He was orange and red,
He made a weird sound that sounded like *'Boo!'*
He tasted like chocolate,
He smelled like toffee,
He looked like Liquorice Allsorts,
He felt like eels,
He reminded me of my mum, all cross with me.

Andrew Clowes (8)
Ackworth Howard CE J&I School

Love

Love is like a small field full of pretty flowers
And newborn lambs leaping around in it.
Love tastes like warm melted chocolate, ready to eat.
Love feels like cuddling a big teddy, when you are feeling down.
Love is light blue like the sky on a beautiful, sunny morning.
Love reminds me of playing with the best friends
Anyone could ever have.

Lily R Vickers (9)
Ackworth Howard CE J&I School

Friendship

Friendship is like one thousand teddies in one bed.
Friendship is the best thing you can get.
Friendship feels like soft velvet.
Friendship tastes like creamy chocolate.
It reminds me of my friends.

George Withington (8)
Ackworth Howard CE J&I School

Light

Light is like a cream cake and the Caribbean sand.
The light is like a woolly white lamb.
It creeps behind silver glittering stars at night.
Light is as heavy as a bird when it takes flight.
Light is electricity, when you turn on the light,
It is always dark in the middle of the night,
If you don't turn on the light.

Jack Roberts (9)
Ackworth Howard CE J&I School

Dragons

D readful dragons
R oaring and very
A ngry
G reen scales, big and small
O ne, two, three dead already
N o one dares
S o just don't dare yourself.

Eleanor Neale (9)
Ackworth Howard CE J&I School

Sadness

Sadness is blue, like ice never melting.
It looks like sad and upset people living on the streets.
It reminds you of the time your great grandmother died.
Sadness sounds like a cry of death and misfortune.
It feels like the end of the world.

Tom Clayton (9)
Ackworth Howard CE J&I School

I Dreamt

I dreamt of a dragon,
With a fiery breath,
I woke up in the morning
And my friend was dead,
Burnt to a crisp like a piece of toast,
Now she's the dragon,
Sunday roast.

I dreamt of a bird,
With a big, sharp beak,
I woke up in the morning
And heard a shriek,
I saw my friend slouched,
Against a door,
A pool of blood on the floor.

I dreamt of a cat,
Who lived in a hat
And funnily, he drank tea,
He made such a fuss when he went on a bus,
Because he had to sit on someone's knee,
The conductor said, 'Puss, stop making a fuss,
Or I will make you get off the bus!'

Annabel Sylvester (10)
Cliff School

Why?

Hand me that book,
Why?
Because I want to look,
Why?
It's all about a cook
Why?
I want to know how to make duck,
Why?
That's what we're having for tea,
Why?
Wait and you will see,
Why?
Before I turn ninety-three,
Why?
Some things aren't meant to be,
Why?
It's just a saying,
Why?
Quit playing,
Why?
You had better start obeying,
Why?

Hayley Brien (10)
Cliff School

Doctor McPockter

Alan McPockter was a famous doctor,
Who travelled all over the world.
One day in France,
He met a guy named Lance,
Who entered a musical show.

After a week he went to the Peaks
And found a packet of sweets.
Up on the mountain,
He saw a big fountain
And wondered if it could leak.

Later on in the day,
He travelled to Pompeii,
To see the volcano blow,
After a while the crowd went wild
And the poor doctor went limping home!

Gayathri Vakkalanka (11)
Cliff School

Question Poem

Am I right or am I wrong?
Does a bell go ding-dong?
Is a bear pink or brown?
What shape is a crown?
Does a window have a frame?
Should I walk down the lane?
What time is 9 o'clock?
How many birds are in a flock?
Is the world round like a ball?
Should I jump down and fall?
Is Japan cold or hot?
How many pencils are in the pot?
Is a chalk black or white?
Does the moon come out at night?
All these questions fill my mind,
But more I seem to find.

Charlotte Hale (11)
Cliff School

Cacklers, Cacklers

The caw of a crow and a giant toad leaping,
The wings of a bat and a little girl shrieking,
The hands of a zombie and the eyes of a cat,
Spiderwebs and the tail of a rat,
The howl of wolves and a slow slug's slime,
The claws of a hawk are still in line,
The toes of a boy and the blood of a unicorn,
An ostrich leg and a rhino-powdered horn,
The brain of a monkey and the heart of a donkey,
The shadows of darkness lying beneath the oak tree,
Deer antlers and fish fins too,
Be careful or witches will be after you.

Lucy Mandelj (10)
Cliff School

My Grandma

My grandma is a squashy chair
And a big yellow sun
And a big chocolate bun.

She is a big fluffy cat
And a floaty balloon,
You have to say, she's as shiny as the moon.

She's as fussy as my mum,
She's as warm as gravy,
My grandma is the best, you see, according to me.

Rhianna Davies (9)
Collingham Lady Hastings CE Primary School

What A Good Footy Match

When I lead my players to the field
No one's cheering for me
Everyone's cheering for Owen

When I score a header,
No one's cheering, not even Mum, Dad or younger brother James
I felt sad inside

What shall I do?
I feel like I'm a beginner
And not a winner

And after the match I hear people talking about how good I played
And people coming and patting me on my back and saying well done
Now I feel happy inside.

Saia Halafihi (8)
Collingham Lady Hastings CE Primary School

There Is A Tree

There is a tree that lives outside
There is a tree that's fat and wide
There is a tree that does high kicks
There is a tree that does the splits
There is a tree that lives inside

There is a tree that's tall and thin
There is a tree that feeds the birds
There is a tree that shelters me
But my favourite tree of all
Is the one at the bottom of my garden
Because it's the tallest of all!

Megan Shaw (8)
Collingham Lady Hastings CE Primary School

Dogs

Have you seen all these dogs running round the park?

Big and fat furry ones
Small and skinny ones
Tall and silly ones
Pink and frizzy ones
Giddy and dizzy ones
Fancy and sporty ones
Wild and smelly ones
Slim and big-bellied ones
Haughty and naughty ones
Dirty and filthy ones.

Can you see all these different dogs?

Finlay Holt (10)
Collingham Lady Hastings CE Primary School

I See An Owl

I see an owl
Sleeping in the day
Twitching its eyes
As white as paper
The shape of an egg
Feathers as soft as a cloud
'Twit-t-woo,' is all it says
Waking, gently for a night of hunting
Swooping off.

Adam Wood (9)
Collingham Lady Hastings CE Primary School

The Kitten

There stands a kitten, all alone
Homeless, lost or abandoned
Left without a home
So sweet and cute.

It stares at me
I feel so sorry
I really feel so helpless
I know I have to come back later.

I go back home
Then come back later
My mum brings a blanket
I wrap it in the blanket.

I bring it home and feed it
It eats like a lion
Then goes to sleep
I take it to the RSPCA.

Two days later, a home was found
I was glad I helped!

Elizabeth Timperley (8)
Collingham Lady Hastings CE Primary School

Counting

Counting, counting, one, two, three,
Easy peasy it is for me,
Four, five, six, seven, eight, nine,
I find it easy all the time.

Ten, eleven, twelve and thirteen,
Keep on counting and getting keen,
Fourteen, fifteen, sixteen, seventeen, eighteen, nineteen,
When I get to twenty, I think I've done plenty.

Caitlin Rose Duffy (7)
Collingham Lady Hastings CE Primary School

Dreams

I embrace the darkness,
Enter worlds,
Where life disappears
And my own world unfurls.

Where I can dance with the dolphins,
Sing with the trees,
Sanity of Earth just evaporates
And I'm there, but no one sees.

I can laugh with the wind,
Joke with the fire
And discuss with the water.

The snow-topped peaks of mountain ranges,
The bottom of the deepest sea,
I can see the world from another's eyes
And no one can disrupt me.

Dreams are your own,
I live mine,
Live yours.

Callum Kenny (11)
Collingham Lady Hastings CE Primary School

The Yellow Mac Head Teacher

There was a head teacher at Stoke,
Who had a very bad stroke,
So when he came back,
He wore a yellow Mac
And drank a bottle of coke.

Sally Eardley (10)
Collingham Lady Hastings CE Primary School

Sweets

Into the sweet shop I go,
What to choose?
I don't know

Gobstoppers here
Lollies there
Sweets are standing
Everywhere

Tins and jars stand in a row
Full of sweets, there on show
What to choose?
What to have?
Shall I have a lucky bag?

Mars bars, Snickers, Milky Ways!
I could be choosing here for days!

Kieren Wilson (9)
Collingham Lady Hastings CE Primary School

I See A Dog

I see a dog
Sprinting, chasing a ball
Fast as a bullet, shooting
The fudgy colours shooting everywhere
Long and thin, like a sausage
Smooth, sleek fur
Barking loud and clear
Prancing through the bushes
I see my dog sleeping in its bed.

Lydia Houseman (9)
Collingham Lady Hastings CE Primary School

Homework!

Homework! Homework!
Every day
I wish at school I could just
Play.

I like to sit and just chatter
Does school really matter?
Come on children,
There's that sound.
The teacher tells us to
Settle down!
Pens and paper,
Put them down!

I sit and stare at the board,
I hate school, I'm really bored.

'Tonight's homework,'
I hear her say,
Homework, homework, every day.

Lauren Wilson (9)
Collingham Lady Hastings CE Primary School

My Dog, Alice

A cute black, white and brown Border collie
L ovely and friendly and very playful
I love her *soooooo* much
C an pull you when you take her out
E very dog is cute, but not as cute as mine.

Kerry Waite (10)
Collingham Lady Hastings CE Primary School

Mystery Book

There's a book on the shelf,
It's a mystery to me,
No one's ever read it,
No one dares go and see.

There's a book on the shelf,
It's grey and dark and black,
No one's going to handle it,
They're scared it will fight back.

There's a book on the shelf,
Hidden from us all,
Our teacher can't see it,
It's right up tall.

There's a book on the shelf,
That I can't reach,
Oh no, it's the teacher,
She's trying to teach!

Zoë Meek (10)
Collingham Lady Hastings CE Primary School

I Wish

I wish I had a little sister to play with.
I wish there was no school to go to.
I wish there were no adults to boss us kids about.
I wish the world was made of candy for everybody to eat.

I wish I had a dog to play with me.
I wish I had no parents to boss me about.
I wish that I could touch the stars.
I wish that I could fly to Neverland.

Ashleigh Davies (8)
Collingham Lady Hastings CE Primary School

What Am I?

I wag my tail
I chase my ball
I like my food
I have a call.

My call is funny
It sounds like a bark
I love my owners
They take me to the park.

I am a nice creature
I like to sleep
Sometimes I snore
But sometimes I weep.

I am a dog.

Ruth Belchetz (9)
Collingham Lady Hastings CE Primary School

Who Am I?

I'm the sort of person who likes to play on my PS2.
I'm the sort of person who hates to lose something.
Happiness for me, is winning a cup final.
Frightening for me, is playing in the dark.
I'm the sort of person who imagines being a footballer.
I'm the sort of person who wants Leeds United back in the
Premiership!
I dream that one day I'll be like Rooney.
But for now, I'm just *me!*

Jamie Heeley (9)
Collingham Lady Hastings CE Primary School

Smelly Socks

Can you see those smelly socks
In that washing basket?

Horrible, stinky, pongy ones,
Square-shaped, soggy ones,
Damp, plain, boring ones,
Squishy, squelchy, squashy ones,
Green, grey, gross ones,
Short, tight, itchy ones,
Nice, warm, cosy ones.

Can you see those smelly socks
In that washing basket?

Eliot Dixon (9)
Collingham Lady Hastings CE Primary School

Tragedies And War

The trigger pulls, the blood, deep red,
Eight million souls are lying, dead.

There's a blitz in the town,
The houses falling, burning down.

The machine gun stutters,
Kills rats in the gutters.

This blood-thirsty nightmare is never over.
People dead fills my heart with dread.

Callum Barnham & Tom Boyes-Park (9)
Collingham Lady Hastings CE Primary School

Puppies

I have a dog called Buffy
On Wednesday she had four puppies
There are two girls and two boys
In the night they make such a noise
They are squeaking and groping
We are keeping one puppy, we are hoping
A girl or a boy? We can't choose
We told everybody the good news!

Sophie Mirczuk (9)
Collingham Lady Hastings CE Primary School

Who Am I?

I'm the sort of person who likes to play on the trampoline.
I'm the sort of person who hates to fall out with my mum.
Happiness for me, is painting pictures.
Frightening for me, is having bad dreams.
I'm the sort of person who wants curly hair.
I dream that one day I'll never have to wear glasses.
But for now, I'm just *me!*

Maggie Cunningham (8)
Collingham Lady Hastings CE Primary School

Swimming Lover Kennings

Fast swimmer
Heron hater
Fin user
Orange body
Flake eater
Pond liver
Net dodger.

Emily Anne Wood (11)
Collingham Lady Hastings CE Primary School

I Feel Hungry

Woke up, hungry
Got dressed, hungry
Ran down the stairs, hungry.

I feel hungry!

Ate a chocolate bar, hungry
Went to Ma, she gave me a fruity bar, hungry
Drank a Fruit Shoot - had to scoot, fast, hungry.

I feel hungry!

I went to school, hungry
At lunch, ate too much, hungry
Ate so much, I had to rush, not hungry
(It all went down with a flush.)

I feel fine!

Do I feel fine? Hungry
Tummy's empty again, hungry
Dinner time I had pizza.

I feel great!

Rhonwen Powell (8)
Collingham Lady Hastings CE Primary School

My Cat, Pumpkin

My cat Pumpkin chases mice,
He freaks me out, but still, he's nice.

My cat Pumpkin has lots of fur
And if you cuddle him, he starts to purr.

My cat Pumpkin is quite fat,
I love him lots, because he's my cat.

Alice Clews (9)
Collingham Lady Hastings CE Primary School

My Grandad's Star

My grandad's star is in the sky
I really wish that I could fly
Up to the sky
To that bright star
That's so very far
Up in the sky.

If I could fly
Up in the sky
I would say, 'Hi!'
To my grandad
Whose star is so bright
It shines like a million watt light.

It shines so bright
So I can see
That he is watching over me
Up in the sky
Way up high
Oh, how I wish that I could fly!

Oliver Ledingham Smith (11)
Collingham Lady Hastings CE Primary School

Can It Be, Or Can't It?

A ghost glides through the gloomy darkness
Of your deserted kitchen and cellar
And who can tell what he's searching for,
Howling with the noise of the blowing wind.
It can't be a ghost, you say to yourself,
Peering through the window sill,
But the universe outside, is hushed and peaceful.

Ben Horner (10)
Collingham Lady Hastings CE Primary School

Roller Coaster, Roller Coaster

I climb up the hill
Time stands still
My back starts to break
There's a rattle and a shake
There's a churning and a burning
My stomach is turning.

My heart nearly popped
When suddenly we stopped
We had reached the top
My hat wanted to fly
Into the sky.

We raced to the bottom
So fast I felt rotten
My eyes filled with pride
As I finished the ride.

Aileen Maria Duffy (8)
Collingham Lady Hastings CE Primary School

My Cat, Katie

She is a comfy bed,
She is a yellow ray of sun that is always shining,
She is an energetic lamb,
She is the smell of lavender,
She is the sound of the flute tooting away,
A sparkling morning with the sun shining,
She is sweet,
She is a perfect cat!

Hannah Priestley (9)
Collingham Lady Hastings CE Primary School

Who Are They?

Who are they?
They love me so much.
Who are they?
They are soft to touch.

Who are they?
They are clever and smart.
Who are they?
They are good at art.

Who are they?
They are loving and kind.
Who are they?
They have brilliant minds.

Who are they?
They are my
Mum and dad
And I love them.

Jordan Brown (9)
Collingham Lady Hastings CE Primary School

Stationary

Pencils scratch
Rubbers run
Rulers rule
All of us!

Cath Noble (9)
Collingham Lady Hastings CE Primary School

Who Am I?

I'm the sort of person who likes to go swimming.
I'm the sort of person who hates to do nothing.
Happiness for me is to go to school.
Frightening for me is to play football.
I'm the sort of person who imagines I'm a football player
                                                    with a good job.
I'm the sort of person who wants to be a millionaire.
I dream that one day I will be famous.
But for now, I am *me!*

Jamie Edward Lock (9)
Collingham Lady Hastings CE Primary School

No One To Play With

Sitting at the classroom door, watching kids play,
Someone comes up to you and says, 'Do you want to come and play?'
I say, 'Yes please,' then I'm playing army men,
With my new friends,
Then the bell goes and everyone is moaning,
But I say, 'Let's play, next play!'

Elliot Clayton (9)
Collingham Lady Hastings CE Primary School

Izzy

She's a wild, wacky Wally with a whim, wham, woo,
She's a perfect party princess to me and you,
She's got lots of style like most girls do,
She's a dazzling disco diva and you know that's true!

Charlotte l'Anson (9)
Collingham Lady Hastings CE Primary School

Why?

Why?
Why did my friend miss the bus?
Why?
Why did the teacher throw the chalk?
Why?
Why did my dad break the phone?
Why?
Why did my friend miss the goal?
Why?
Why did my nana snore at night?
Why?
Why did I write this poem?
Why? Because we are all human.

Harrison Grange (8)
Collingham Lady Hastings CE Primary School

Going To Sleep

I can hear the fairies dancing
The stars twinkling
The owls hooting
No wonder I can't sleep.

I can hear my mum on the phone
My dad watching TV
My baby brother crying
No wonder I can't sleep.

But now the house is quiet
The fairies have all gone home
The moon is full and shining
Now I think I'll sleep.

Sophie Young (7)
Collingham Lady Hastings CE Primary School

There Was A Young Man

There was a young man who was drunk,
Who was also a bit of a punk,
When he saw any beer,
He gave a massive cheer,
So his bum won't fit on his bunk.

Richard Gorvin (10)
Collingham Lady Hastings CE Primary School

A Limerick

There was a young fellow called Fred
Who always liked to eat dry bread
Bread would make a fine house
But what about the mouse?
Then he made a leaded shed instead.

Sarah Whitla (11)
Collingham Lady Hastings CE Primary School

Mrs Barnes

She's a tulip, big and strong
She's yellow, bouncy and jolly,
She's a nice, calm, bouncy chair,
An eagle flying overhead, peering at everyone,
She's a morning type of person,
A piece of double chocolate cake
And that's Mrs Barnes!

Abie Roberts (9)
Collingham Lady Hastings CE Primary School

Spotted Predator Kennings

Spotted hider
Speedy runner
Flashy pouncer
Powerful biter
Sharp scratcher
Paw printer.

Chris Lyons (11)
Collingham Lady Hastings CE Primary School

I Saw A Cat

I saw a cat.
I saw a big cat.
I saw a big, fat cat.
I saw a big, fat, ugly cat.
But everyone knows that
The big, fat, ugly cat, is my cat.

Graeme Duffy (7)
Collingham Lady Hastings CE Primary School

Mysterious Person Kennings

Head chopper
Leg lobber
Heart stabber
Disguise master
Police runner
Life destroyer.

George Grange (10)
Collingham Lady Hastings CE Primary School

Bedtime

When it's dark and I go to bed
Thousands of thoughts
Pop up in my head.
Questions, more questions
What, where and why?
Can you answer these questions?
How do birds fly?
How far is Mars?
Is the moon made of cheese?
How fast does blood flow?
Can you answer that please?
And just when I'm thinking
I start counting sheep
And in no time at all
I find I'm asleep.

Ross Goddard (9)
Collingham Lady Hastings CE Primary School

My Cat

My cat
Lives on a mat
He plays with his ball
Under the hall
He goes to sleep
In a big heap
On his mat
There's a baseball bat
My cat.

Harry Akitt (7)
Collingham Lady Hastings CE Primary School

Spaghetti

S oft and slippery in a
P ool of tomato sauce
A lways my favourite, so
G ood to gobble up
H appy it makes me at
E very occasion
T oo yummy to waste at
T ea, lunch or dinner
I love spaghetti, it's always a winner!

Robbie Eardley (8)
Collingham Lady Hastings CE Primary School

Capture

I want to capture the sound of the beautiful birds singing.
I want to capture the feel of the rough prickle on my skin.
I want to capture the smell of the red rose in the garden.
I want to capture the sight of the soft, furry cat.
I want to capture the taste of the hard, delicious chocolate.
I want to capture the moment when the dog was running to me.
I want to capture the memory of when I was a baby.
I want to capture the silence of the dog sleeping.
I want to capture the feeling of the soft, cuddly bear.

Ellie May Clark (7)
Gawthorpe JI & N School

My Abstract Poem

I would love to hear the swaying of the seaweed
as it gently moves on the seabed,
or the bluebells tinkering in the lush green wood
under the tree, which is swaying in the wind.

I should like to taste a small piece of the enormous moon
to see if it was made out of cheese,
or the rough bark of an ancient oak tree.

I would just love to catch the first white, patterned snowflake,
which I could hold in my hand and would never melt
so I could save it forever,
also to stand next to the hot blazing sun,
so I can feel how warm it is on my cheek.

I would like to smell the cold wind on a cool winter's day
and a fluffy white puff of a cloud in a clear blue sky
surrounded by other clouds,
I should like to see the air that is wrapped around us.

Emily Layton (10)
Gawthorpe JI & N School

Untitled

I should like to see a soft, calm, silky bear laying down with its babies.
I should like to hear a sleepy tiger moaning so quietly in his
peaceful sleep.
I would like to feel the soft touch of a fairy's wing, so smooth and silky.
I would like to taste the rich, bitter taste of smooth saltwater,
fresh from the ocean.
I should like to smell a fresh, sweet toffee, new from the wrapper.
I would like to capture the moment when a stinging bee
has its first sting and its little munchkin body disappears.
I would like to capture the feeling of a little teddy bear just being made
with silky fabrics and lots of little stitches beneath his feet.
I would like to capture the memory of my friends just being born
and the first words they ever gargled.

Alice Scales (10)
Gawthorpe JI & N School

The Magic Box

(Based on 'Magic Box' by Kit Wright)

I will put in my magic box the crackling sound of the leaves
on the floor in autumn,
The sound of the children laughing out loud,
The sound of a baby crying,
A Chinese whisper in the air.

I will put in my magic box a child's smile
looking straight at you,
Seeing a little fish trying to jump out of the lake,
Seeing a twinkling drop of snow, dropping on the floor,
Even to see an ocean view straight out of the window.

I will put in my magic box the fresh smell of roses in my garden,
Some perfume on the day I go out,
The smell of a new car freshener in my car.

I will leave my magic box open for everyone to see with their hearts.

Brogan Gale (10)
Gawthorpe JI & N School

My Magic Imaginations

I would love to hear the fluttering of a fairy's delicate wings,
as they sparkle and twinkle in the night sky.

I would adore seeing the sparkling and shimmering of the night sky,
as I get ready for bed.

I should like to feel the sparkling of a star's points
as it relaxes in the night sky.

I would rather taste the dark twinkling night sky,
than the misty winter's air.

I would like to capture the scary memory
of my first day at school.

Chloé Jaye Ottewell (10)
Gawthorpe JI & N School

Senses

I would like to hear the moon roaring across the night sky,
Also, to hear the Mona Lisa snoozing in her frame.

I should like to see the sound of an electric eel letting off sparks,
Or a magnificent eagle squawking in a clear blue sky.

I should like to smell freshly baked bread coming from the oven
And fresh washing hung on the line.

I would like to taste a fruit juice rainbow in the clear blue sky,
Also a bird's song floating on the breeze.

I should like to smell the smoky sun setting over the horizon,
Or the watery sky turning into night.

I would like to capture the moment when I first heard
My baby step-cousin talk.

I should like to capture the feeling
Of always knowing someone's there for you.

I would like to capture the memory
Of my first goal for my football team.

Jordan Crosland (10)
Gawthorpe JI & N School

Capture

I want to capture the sound of Miss Adams shouting.
I want to capture the feel of my dad playing with my hair.
I want to capture the smell of my dad when he comes home from work.
I want to capture the sight of the big waves in Cornwall.
I want to capture the taste of melting chocolate on my tongue.
I want to capture the moment when my dad cuddles me.
I want to capture the memory of when my hamster died.
I want to capture the silence of my mum and dad messing.
I want to capture the feeling of when it is Christmas.

Amy Watson (8)
Gawthorpe JI & N School

I Would Like To Feel . . .

I wish I could see the golden fairy dust
sprinkling over the peaceful, white daisies,
Or I would like to capture the feeling of an artist's paintings
the creation of how he feels.

I should like to feel the fluffy afro mane of a wild African lion
And the coldness of the moon making a chalky light in the sky
on a mid-spring's night.

I would like to smell the bright lemony sun
glazing in the cloudless, blue sky,
Or the freshness of a cold winter's morning
with frost covering my doorstep.

I wish I could taste the fruity, sweet colours of the rainbow,
Or the clashing of the black thunder.

Megan Crabtree (11)
Gawthorpe JI & N School

Fear And Excitement

Fear
Fear is black,
It smells like the sea drowning over me,
Fear tastes dry and sour,
It sounds like thudding heartbeats,
It feels cold and wet,
Fear lives on the clouds above.

Excitement
Excitement is yellow,
It smells fresh and radiant,
Excitement tastes sweet and nice,
It sounds like laughter and applause,
It feels bouncy and bumpy,
Excitement lives in our hearts and minds.

Courtnie Calcutt (11)
Gawthorpe JI & N School

My Magic Box

(Based on 'Magic Box' by Kit Wright)

I will put in my box . . .
The ducklings squawking along the wavy water.
The frogs jumping from lily pad to lily pad in the wavering water.
The jingling of the sleigh when Santa arrives.

I will put in my box . . .
The smell of strawberries on a summer's day.
The smell of rain on an autumn day.
The smell of candyfloss while walking through the fair.

I will put in my box . . .
The taste of chocolate cake
All spongy in your mouth,
Or the hard toffee crackling in your mouth.

I will put in my box . . .
The twinkling of fairy lights on my Christmas tree
And the sight of a beautiful rainbow when the sun and rain meet.
The first sparkling snowdrop on the ground.

I will put in my box . . .
The feel of an elephant's skin, all rough and wrinkly.
Or the feel of a baby's bottom, all soft and gentle
And the feel of a fish's skin, all slimy and scaly.

I will leave my box open for everyone to see,
Twenty-four hours a day,
Seven days a week.

Joanne Rourke (10)
Gawthorpe JI & N School

The Magic Box

(Based on 'Magic Box' by Kit Wright)

I will put in the box . . .
The smell of a roast dinner cooking in the oven.
The smell of brand new leather shoes on the first day back at school.
The smell of roses on a hot summer's day.

I will put in the box . . .
The taste of icy ice cream, slowly melting down my throat.
The taste of chewy Christmas cake, laced with boozy brandy.

I will put in the box . . .
The touch of the lovely velvet from the quilt cover on my bed.
The touch of a lovely rabbit, its fur softly touching your cheek.
The touch of lovely Christmas presents all wrapped up.

I will put in the box . . .
The sight of a red and pink sunset setting over the sparkling water.
The children playing noisily, swinging and shouting.
The dogs playing with other dogs, running around excitedly.

I will leave my box open to let all that arrive
Touch and feel it
And the blind and the deaf
And different cultures are welcome too.
The box is not just for me,
But also for you.

Nathan Sorby (11)
Gawthorpe JI & N School

The Magic Box

(Based on 'Magic Box' by Kit Wright)

I will put in the box . . .
The smell of a roast dinner cooking in the oven.
The smell of brand new leather shoes on the first day back at school.
The smell of roses on a hot summer's day.

I will put in the box . . .
The taste of icy ice cream slowly melting down my throat.
The taste of chewy Christmas cake laced with boozy brandy.
The sip of steaming hot coffee on a cold winter's day.

I will put in the box . . .
The feel of the sand sinking under my feet.
The feel of the sea going on the tip of your toes.
The feel of a baby's wet hair on the tips of your fingers.

I will leave it open so everyone can see in it around the world.

Christopher Skevington (11)
Gawthorpe JI & N School

War And Peace

War
War is lava-red,
It smells like smoke coming from a fired cannon.
War tastes like smoke in your lungs,
It sounds like gunshots in the distance,
It feels like fire burning to the ground,
War lives in the depths of the darkest forest.

Peace
Peace is bright yellow,
It smells like fresh air in the morning,
Peace tastes like melted chocolate,
It sounds like birds singing,
It feels smooth and soft,
Peace lives in the middle of your heart.

Christian Reddyhoff (10)
Gawthorpe JI & N School

I Would Love To . . .

I would love to capture the sound of a trickling, rocky,
Gentle waterfall in the cold, windy morning
And I would like to keep the sound of a beautiful rainbow
Forming in the hot summer's sky.

I would love to feel a crowd of shooting stars
Gently passing by the glowing moon on a freezing winter's night.

I would like to smell the scent of the sun's scalding core
And capture it forever,
Also the amazing power of my first flight.

I should love to taste the calm air,
Which floats around our air in the autumn wind,
Also the smell of an axe forced into a tree.

Daniel Rooney (11)
Gawthorpe JI & N School

I Would Like To . . .

I would like to hear the calm, peaceful, full, blazing orange sunset,
Behind the green, spiky, giant hill, under the orange hazy sky.

I should love to see a falling, bright, glittery star on a winter's night,
Shooting into my warm white gloves.

I would like to feel a blue warm cow in a green, grassy field,
Or the grass on a warm summery day.

I should like to taste all the colours of the beautiful bright rainbow,
Just appearing on a hot, drizzly day.

Dale Treloar (11)
Gawthorpe JI & N School

Magic Box

(Based on 'Magic Box' by Kit Wright)

I will put in my box . . .
The sight of England scoring in Euro 2004,
My cat rolling over and jumping on my knee,
The view from my nan's backyard.

I will put in my box . . .
The sound of the birds singing when you wake up,
The sound of fireworks on Bonfire Night,
The sound of the sea lapping on the sand.

I will put in my box . . .
The taste of a crispy Mars Delight,
The taste of a really warm dish of stew and dumplings,
The taste of a Sunday dinner melting in your mouth.

I will leave my box open so everybody can feel free to look inside.

Robert Wilson (11)
Gawthorpe JI & N School

Chance

I wish I could feel the brightness of the stormy
And never-ending floating night.
I want to have the chance to hear all the noisy
Planets of the freezing, foggy universe.
Also, I really want to capture the sound of
Nature's smooth and quiet songs of her forest friends.
I would like to see a sunset's blazing, bright
Reflection on the silky, calm water of the Mississippi.
Plus, I want to see the future that I can grab
And put into a magical box.

Matthew Kitchen (9)
Gawthorpe JI & N School

The Magic Box

(Based on 'Magic Box' by Kit Wright)

I will put in the box . . .
The duckling squeaking in the wavy water,
The frogs jumping on each lily pad in the wavy water,
The cat miaowing in the night.

I will put in the box . . .
Poppies blowing in the wind,
Children playing with their toys at Christmas,
The fairy on top of a Christmas tree, granting wishes.

I will put in the box . . .
A piece of hot sponge pudding, sizzling in the oven,
Chocolate melting in a pan,
A Christmas pudding set on fire.

I will put in the box . . .
A hot pepperoni pizza, hot and spicy,
Hot chips in oil,
A red-hot fire on a black night.

I will keep the box open so everyone can see,
People from Bora Bora to England.

Laura-Molly Walker (11)
Gawthorpe JI & N School

Capture

I want to capture the sound of the radio in my bedroom.
I want to capture the feel of my cousin's cat.
I want to capture the smell of melting Smarties in my mouth.
I want to capture the sight of beautiful birds singing in the trees.
I want to capture the taste of sea salt.
I want to capture the memory of when I fell off my chair.
I want to capture the moment when I fell off my skateboard.
I want to capture the sight of when I made a bun.
I want to capture the feeling of a fluffy bed.

Oliver Brown (8)
Gawthorpe JI & N School

World Senses

I would like to taste the beautiful colours of the rainbow,
each tasting like tropical citrus fruits.

I would like to touch a soft unicorn's back,
riding carefree across fields,
which have emerald-green, glistening grass.

I would like to hear the dew on a frosty,
almost-at-the-end, autumn morning,
a tinkling bell sound every time it moves.

I need to see the fresh clean wind,
or a yawn of a hippopotamus.

Wind would look so colourful
and a yawn would look like pink squiggly lines.

I would love to taste history, or bittersweet revenge.
History would taste brown and crumbly
and revenge, sour like a lime.

I would like to touch hate or maybe victory.
Hate would be rough like an electric shock
and victory would be soft and fluffy, but still tough.

I need to hear the future or the past.
The future like a robot's beep
and the past like a dinosaur's roar.

Natalie Summerscales (9)
Gawthorpe Jl & N School

The Magic Box

(Based on 'Magic Box' by Kit Wright)

I will put in my box . . .
The smell of roses blossoming in the summer,
The smell of fish and chips that have come straight from the fish shop,
The smell of the roast dinner that has come out of the oven.

I will put in my box . . .
The sound of the bells of Santa Claus,
The sound of violins playing nice sounds,
The sound of the leaves crunching upon the ground.

I will put in my box . . .
The taste of the curry from the delivery man,
The taste of roast tatties, all nice and hot,
The taste of the cookies with chocy bits on them.

I will put in my box . . .
The sight of the birds upon the tree,
The sight of the children playing in the street,
The sight of the dogs barking in the garden.

I will put in my box . . .
The touch of the snow sprinkling on the grass,
The touch of the wrapping paper on a present,
The touch of the cat's fur curling around your legs.

Chloe Dewhirst (10)
Gawthorpe JI & N School

My Abstract Poem

I would like to hear a shooting star moving
quickly across the sky.
Or a snowflake the colour of a white fluffy cloud
floating towards me.
I should like to see a lake drifting back and forth
after a violent, windy day.
I should like to feel the hot summer slowly changing
to autumn, overnight.
I would like to feel the texture of the silky, elegant sand
going through my fingers.
I would like to taste a sugary sweet jam biscuit
from Mars,
or a chocolate-coated, rich, slick marshmallow
that's just been toasted.
I would capture the moment of a newborn baby
at its first Christmas.

Eleanor Burkinshaw (9)
Gawthorpe JI & N School

Magic Box

(Based on 'Magic Box' by Kit Wright)

I will put in the magic box . . .
The smell of freshly baked bread in the bakers,
I will put in the box the smell of a burning fire on a winter's night.

I will put in the magic box . . .
The taste of a chicken wing, crisp when you bite into it,
The taste of Christmas pudding tingling in my mouth,
Chocolate cake as spongy as a sponge,
Nuts that break in my mouth, like an acorn falling from a tree.

I will put in the magic box . . .
The ears of a meerkat,
The sound of the fireworks on Bonfire Night,
The sound of whales calling to each other,
The first touch of a feather off a swan,
The scales of a snake and a pillow of a new sofa.

Alexander Green (10)
Gawthorpe JI & N School

Untitled

I would like to hear the sound of a calm, beautiful waterfall flowing,
Or a flower as it blooms.
I would like to see my best friends,
Or a rainbow sat upon the clouds.
I would like to taste the heavenly, rich taste of Galaxy chocolate,
Also the crunch of a chocolate Smartie cookie.
I would like to feel the warm breeze blowing on my face,
Or to be so tall I could see the whole Earth.
I should like to smell the deep smell of a rose,
Or a big chocolate cake baking in the oven.
I would like to capture the moment when I open
The biggest Christmas present ever made,
Or on all my friends' birthdays when they blow out all the candles.
I would like to capture the feeling of everybody smiling,
Or my best friends and family having fun.
I would like to capture the memory of the best Christmas
And the best birthday I have ever had.

Alice Ramsden (10)
Gawthorpe JI & N School

The Magic Box

(Based on 'Magic Box' by Kit Wright)

I will put in the box . . .
A red and orange sunset setting on the sea.
The fairy lights twinkling on the Christmas tree.
A colourful rainbow stretching across the sky.

I will put in the box . . .
The smell of freshly ground coffee wafting through the air.
The smell of freshly baked bread straight from the oven.
The smell of freshly baked cookies.

I will put in the box . . .
A gust of wind blowing in the trees.

Jonathon Wilson (9)
Gawthorpe JI & N School

The Magic Box

(Based on 'Magic Box' by Kit Wright)

I will put in the box . . .
The smell of a roast dinner cooking in the oven,
The smell of brand new shoes on the first day back at school,
The smell of roses on a hot, summer's day.

I will put in the box . . .
The taste of icy ice cream slowly melting down my throat,
The taste of chewy Christmas cake, laced with boozy brandy,
The sip of steaming hot coffee on a cold day.

I will put in the box . . .
The sound of fireworks going *bang, bang,*
The sound of a flute playing,
The sound of children playing.

I will put in the box . . .
The feel of a small, furry animal,
The feel of Christmas paper,
The feel of soft, cotton wool.

I will put in the box . . .
A picture of the blue sky,
A picture of a rainbow across the sky,
A picture of people playing,
Then I will go and show everyone my box.

Kimberley Harris (10)
Gawthorpe JI & N School

The Magic Box

(Based on 'Magic Box' by Kit Wright)

I will put in the box . . .
A red and orange sunset, setting on the sea
The fairy lights twinkling on the Christmas tree
A colourful rainbow stretching across the sky.

I will put in the box . . .
The smell of freshly ground coffee wafting through the air
The smell of freshly baked bread, straight from the oven
The smell of lush, green grass on a summery day.

I will put in the box . . .
The taste of a hot, Christmas dinner on a big plate
The taste of chocolate fudge melting in my mouth
The taste of strawberries and cream on a Christmas night.

I will put in the box . . .
Touching a horse's smooth, velvety fur
Touching a sheep's woolly coat
Touching a ferret's smooth fur.

I will put in the box . . .
The sound of wind blowing
The sound of a rooster's cock-a-doodle-do
The sound of a cow's moo
I will keep my box open for the senseless
To smell, see, taste, feel and hear.

Liam Ward (10)
Gawthorpe JI & N School

The Magic Box

(Based on 'Magic Box' by Kit Wright)

I will put in the box . . .
The smell of a roast dinner cooking in the oven.
The smell of brand new leather shoes on the first day back at school.
The smell of roses on a hot summer's day.

I will put in the box . . .
The taste of icy ice cream slowly melting down my throat.
The taste of a chewy Christmas cake laced with boozy brandy.
The sip of steaming hot coffee on a cold winter's day.

I will put in the box . . .
The drip-drop of silk rain dripping off my window sill.
A sparkly firework shooting up into the shiny bright stars.
The sound of shiny stars flowing out of the baby-blue sky.

I will put in the box . . .
A picture of a mum rocking her baby to sleep.
A picture of a rainbow stretching across the sky.
A picture of children playing and dancing to rock music.

Lauren Smith (10)
Gawthorpe JI & N School

Capture

I want to capture the sound of the bluebirds singing in the morning.
I want to capture the feel of the small crumbs of sand in my shoes.
I want to capture the smell of the delicious sweet cake.
I want to capture the sight of the joyful children on the grass.
I want to capture the taste of the juicy roast beef in my mouth.
I want to capture the moment when the room is nice and calm.
I want to capture the memory of my family.
I want to capture the silence of the early morning.
I want to capture the feeling of my family being happy every day.

Zoe Sheard (8)
Gawthorpe JI & N School

The Magic Box

(Based on 'Magic Box' by Kit Wright)

I will put in my box . . .
The taste of chips with salt settling in my mouth
The taste of a toffee apple crunching in-between my teeth
The taste of a banana, mushy and yellow.

I will put in the box . . .
The touch of freshly laundered clothes
The touch of a special person's hug when I am feeling down
The touch of a camel's fur.

I will put in the box . . .
A beautiful silk sari swaying in the breeze
A rugby ball being passed around
A dragon's breath.

I will put in the box . . .
An electric eel swimming in rivers, swimming and splashing
A classroom full of children working
A baby's first words.

Joel Driver (10)
Gawthorpe JI & N School

Capture!

I want to capture the sound of rain tapping on the dry road.
I want to capture the feel of my baby sister's silky skin.
I want to capture the smell of baking bread,
Steaming in the tiny corner of the bakery.
I want to capture the sight of balloons swaying in the breeze.
I want to capture the taste of hot salmon in jiggly hollandaise sauce.
I want to capture the moment when my sister was born.
I want to capture the memory of playing tennis with my friends.
I want to capture the silence of Remembrance Day
When the soldiers stopped.
I want to capture the feeling of happiness when I was really happy.

Jack Hayman (8)
Gawthorpe JI & N School

Magic Box

(Based on 'Magic Box' by Kit Wright)

I will put in my box . . .
The lovely smell of roses
The smell of freshly baked chocolate cake
The smell of a barbeque on a hot summer's evening.

I will put in the box . . .
The sound of a colourful carnival with drums banging
And people singing and dancing.
Baby birds tweeting for their mums
A baby's first words.

I will put in my box . . .
The touch of the sun shining down
When I'm sunbathing on the grass
The touch of a fuzzy, fluffy bunny
The touch of soft, silky sand.

I will put in my box . . .
The taste of mouth-watering hot chocolate
The taste of Christmas pudding
The taste of a chicken having a cha-cha slide.

I will put in my box . . .
The sight of a shark
The sight of the clear sky
The night vision of a bat flying as high as the moon.

Damien Cresswell (10)
Gawthorpe JI & N School

The Magic Box

(Based on 'Magic Box' by Kit Wright)

I will put in my box . . .
The taste of a sticky toffee apple
The taste of a really icy ice cream
The taste of a really nice chocolate melting in my mouth.

I will put in my box . . .
The sound of a colourful carnival with drums banging
And people singing and dancing
Baby birds tweeting for their mums
A baby's first words.

I will put in my box . . .
The fluffy fur on my rabbit
The cold white ice melting in my hand
My fresh clothes when I have just washed them
And they smell so clean.

I will put in my box . . .
The smell of roses on a hot summer's afternoon
The smell of pizza cooking in the oven
The smell of chicken cooking on the stove
I will leave my box open for the whole world to see,
Blind, deaf, everyone and me.

Laura Gomersall (9)
Gawthorpe JI & N School

The Magic Box

(Based on 'Magic Box' by Kit Wright)

I will put in the box . . .
A calm and gentle farm
A beautiful ocean wave
A silent countryside walk.

I will put in the box . . .
The sound of a cockerel crowing
The sound of a kitten purring
The sound of the wind blowing.

I will put in the box . . .
The taste of chocolate melting in my mouth
Summer fruits - strawberries, cherries and pineapple,
Juicy on my tongue
The taste of my mum's Sunday dinner.

I will put in the box . . .
The sight of an eagle flying
A horse running across an empty field
A dog's tail wagging happily.

I will put in the box . . .
The story of my life which I have only just begun.

Charlotte Williamson (9)
Gawthorpe Jl & N School

The Magic Box

(Based on 'Magic Box' by Kit Wright)

I will put in the box . . .
A red and orange sunset setting on the sea
The fairy lights twinkling on the Christmas tree
A colourful rainbow stretching across the sky.

I will put in the box . . .
The smell of freshly ground coffee wafting through the air
The smell of freshly baked bread straight from the oven
The smell of the bonfire on an autumn night
The smell of the Christmas cake.

I will put in the box . . .
The birds singing a song on a summer's day
The Christmas lights shining on the tree
The swan on the soft ground.

I will put in the box . . .
The taste of chewy toffee
The taste of chocolate melting in my mouth
A cup of hot chocolate on a cold winter's night.

I will put in the box . . .
The feel of an animal's silky fur
The soft hair of a newborn child
I will leave my box open for the whole world to see.

Catherine Morton (9)
Gawthorpe JI & N School

Untitled

I would like to see a great, live band in an enormous stadium,
with screaming, obsessed crowds from 30 years ago,
Or see the last, enormous, angry dinosaur fall to the ground
before the freezing Ice Age.

I wish that I could taste every flavour of ice cream in a row
on a freezing ice cream planet,
Or have an everlasting feast in the puffy, white clouds.

I would like to feel the multicoloured rainbow and put it in an oak box
and touch a glittering gold star from the sky.

I'd love to smell an old bunch of lovely flowers from the Tudor times,
Also, to smell the lovely rainbow on a beautiful, golden sunset.

I would like to capture the moment when a terrifying witch
casts her spells,
Or when a baby's first tooth appears.

I would like to capture the feeling of when I opened my first present,
Also when I saw a French eclipse.

I would like to capture the memory of going on holiday for the first time,
Or flying far for the first time.

Cameron Burns (9)
Gawthorpe JI & N School

Capture!

I want to capture the sound of my mum and dad talking happily.
I want to capture the feel of the smooth, soft sand.
I want to capture the smell of Smarties melting.
I want to capture the sight of the beautiful birds singing.
I want to capture the taste of melting ice cream.
I want to capture the moment when I was playing
On my fantastic PS2.
I want to capture the memory of when I was playing rugby.
I want to capture the silence of everyone working.
I want to capture the feeling of my mum, dad and sister
Smiling at me.

Andrew Rourke (8)
Gawthorpe JI & N School

My Poem

I would like to hear the sound of trees' leaves gently swaying
in time with the wind,
Or the sound of people's voices singing in the wind.

I would like to see the sight of an owl's soft *twit-twoo* in the night sky,
Or the feel of a vicious, wild wind in the midnight sky.

I would like to taste a milky, smooth, rich, sweet chocolate
melting in my warm mouth.

I should like to smell the misty, foggy smell of a bonfire burning.

I would like to capture the moment when a newborn baby bird
flies for the first time.

I would like to capture the exciting feeling of Christmas Eve,
Or a shooting star in a midnight sky!

Emma Dixon (9)
Gawthorpe JI & N School

Capture!

I want to capture the sound of fireworks crashing on an autumn night.
I want to capture the feel of furry tree leaves on a hot day.
I want to capture the smell of fresh bread from the bakery.
I want to capture the sight of my big brown dog
Running up and down the field.
I want to capture the moment when my brother will turn his light off
At bedtime.
I want to capture the memory of when I got my fluffy rabbit.
I want to capture the silence of Poppy Day,
When we remember the soldiers who died in the poppy fields.
I want to capture the feeling of when I'm glad I've done my homework.

James Heighton (9)
Gawthorpe JI & N School

Why Me?

Children hide,
Children seek,
Children scream as he comes through the gate.

Children run,
Children get inside,
Children are safe, but me, I came in late.

I am scared,
I am shivering,
I am his new meal,
He comes towards me,
Screaming down my ear,
Playtime was bye-time for me.

The beating, the bashing,
Made me do stupid things,
Skive school,
Shout at my best mate,
I regret that now,
Why did I take it out on her?

But . . .
Whose lunchbox did he throw on the floor?
Whose face did he bash against the wall?
Whose life did he make a misery?
Me.
Why me?

Elisha Merriman (11)
Manston Primary School

The Bully

Like a big silver drop of water,
A tear drops down the new boy's face.
As the bully walks away,
Laughing with his friends.
The new boy stands on his own,
Hurt.

The new boy looks around,
For a friend.
Everybody in a group,
Playing, laughing, smiling.
If only he had a friend,
He wishes.

The bully watches as the new boy goes home,
His mind ticking for when
He is going to see him again,
Tomorrow!
The smile on his face,
He just can't wait.

The new boy gets out of the car,
His feet dragging,
Like there's tons of steel on them,
The sweat dripping down his face,
His hands, trembling.

Shelby Douglas (11)
Manston Primary School

It Hurts!

It hurts when he hits me and when he shouts
And calls me names,
His voice is a microphone belching in my ear.

He takes my lunch away,
I'm hungry,
I'm in his power because I'm small and defenceless.

I can't face it anymore,
It's just locked inside me,
If I don't tell anybody,
It'll be there forever
And will never go away.

I'm fed up with hiding, I'll have to tell someone,
Because if I don't,
Nothing will get done about it.

But if I tell,
He'll be onto me even more,
It hurts.

Beth Matthews (11)
Manston Primary School

I'm The Boy

I'm the boy who was covered up,
Like a turtle in its shell.

I'm the boy who never talked,
Because I was too frightened to talk.

I'm the boy who got no lunch,
Because I was too scared to eat.

I'm the boy who got bullied,
But now I am a bully myself.

James Duckworth (10)
Manston Primary School

Sarah's Scared

(Based on the poem by Richard Edwards)

Sarah's scared of things at school,
Sarah's scared of bullies that drool,
Scared of her brother's dark, dim room,
Scared of bullies that will come very soon.

Sarah's scared of big, tough boys,
Sarah's scared of her sister's noise,
Scared of windows, scared of books,
Scared of shadows, scared of crooks.

Scared of her mum, scared of her dad,
Scared of a girl that's completely mad,
Scared of poisonous snakes that bite,
Scared of falling down a pipe.

Sarah's scared of completely showing,
Scared of big bullies knowing,
That she's scared of everything,
How can she hide this when she's ten?

Annabel Riley (10)
Manston Primary School

The Football Bully

The football bully is football crazy
And very good at it too.

He kicks the ball like a real player,
He's the best striker in school.

He might be good at football,
But he picks on people that aren't.

The football bully has lots of fun,
Bullying lots of children.

The children have done nothing wrong.

The bully has made a big mistake,
To bully all those children.

Andrew Horry (10)
Manston Primary School

The Playground Bullies

Trapped all alone in an empty jail,
Crying also with a wail,
People poking, people pointing,
Everybody was shouting.
Calling names and frightful words,
Only when the jail keeper's gone.
Pushing, hurting and also kicking,
While waiting for keeper to come.
Punching, biting, calling names,
Never letting him join the games.
But keeper came
And all escaped without being noticed,
But later jailor went
And people came again,
Pointing, kicking, shouting and also yelling,
Until the whistle blew
And all went in,
But the prisoner, never spoke a word.

James Padmore (11)
Manston Primary School

School Bully

He was as thick as treacle toffee,
As muscly as a gladiator,
As silly as a joke,
As funky as a rock star,
As sneaky as a burglar,
As weird as a mouse playing football,
As tough as a wrestler
And he was only a baby!

He kicked his mum,
He nipped his dad,
He had so much fun being bad,
But in the end everyone always agrees,
He's only a baby!

Georgina Price (11)
Manston Primary School

The Bully

Like a lump of steel,
The bully moves forward, towards the new boy.
The new boy frets and tries to run,
But the bully grabs him
And his fist goes *thump, thump, thump.*

While the new boy staggers home,
The bully stops laughing and stares,
His conscience talking away,
His heart going *thump, thump, thump.*

When the bully tries to walk away,
His feet are lumps of lead,
He is stuck,
His brain going *thump, thump, thump.*

As the bully walks through the school gate,
He hears cheering, clapping, shouting and laughter,
A huddle of people are gathered around two people,
There's a new bully in town.

Lynsey Beaumont (11)
Manston Primary School

The Bully

James sits on the bench,
Head hung in his hands,
Tears streaming down his face,
Each tear stings his eyes,
As everybody points and laughs
And says, 'Look at him.'
As he wipes the tears from his eyes,
He sees it,
The bully.
As James takes a large gasp
And peers up at the mountain in distress.

Alex Proctor (11)
Manston Primary School

The Man's View

Me, the old man, feeling guilty,
Seeing teenagers out of my window,
Battering small children,
On a sunny morning.
I open the window,
Listening to racist comments
About his colour,
Sounds of screams and thumps.
If they knew, I knew
They would be cowards,
It might even stop them,
But I have no idea where he lives.
The boy half the age of the bully
Having no chance of winning,
Feeling sad and scared in his heart.
One day they'll find out
And get punished,
Maybe get into trouble with the law.

Joseph Cooney (11)
Manston Primary School

Only The Sun Knew

(Based on a poem by Matthew Sweeney)

Only the sun knew that day
When the bully came,
Punching, kicking and thumping,
Like a ferocious bull striking its first prey,
Only the sun knew.

Only the sun knew that day,
The nasty name the bully spoke,
As the terror ran down his face like a ghost's,
Disgrace and humiliation were set free,
Like a pack of hungry lions getting let out of their cages,
Only the sun knew.

Holly Anna Robinson (11)
Manston Primary School

Scaredy-Cat

I'd walk to school every day,
When I hear the sound of children play
And I see my bullies jump out and say,
'Scaredy-cat, scaredy-cat, just go away!'

The children stare and stare
Like the sun over our heads,
While my bullies kick everywhere,
It goes on every day,
'Scaredy-cat, scaredy-cat, just go away!'

A little kid from Year 8,
Who used to be my best mate,
Was playing on a scooter,
Then went to the head teacher
Who was on his computer.

The head teacher had their parents in
And they sorted it all out,
So there was no more,
'Scaredy-cat, scaredy-cat, just go away!'

Chelsea Lee Holmes (10)
Manston Primary School

Scared

As I walk, people call me names.
As I walk, people shove and push me.
As I watch the ferocious devils approach,
I hide in the shadows.

I see the sign that the devil is here
As he waves his stick,
The glow of red in his eyes,
The laugh of death is here and I fear I am next.

Aimee L Routledge (10)
Manston Primary School

The Big Bullies

Bullies are like toffee,
They stick to you until you die,
Bullies are like icing,
Covering things up inside,
Bullies bully with pride,
But somewhere inside they have all got to decide,
Whether they're right or wrong.

Bullies make you feel like jelly,
So they can show off all their stunts
That they watched on telly.

Bullies are like steel,
They pretend that nothing hurts them,
They pretend that seeing people crying
Does not hurt them,
But inside everyone there's a heart that beats,
So no one can say that nothing hurts them,
Because everyone gets hurt sometimes.

Jade Louise Towers (11)
Manston Primary School

You And I

I like to play,
You like to call people names,
I like to skip,
You like to push people about,
I like to play football,
You like to threaten people,
I would like you to stop bullying,
You will stop some day.

Joe Bilbey (11)
Manston Primary School

The Bully

The bully came to school again,
To fight, punch and kick.
His arms are made of metal,
That always go *click, click.*

Hitting children,
Calling names,
Beating and punching,
Are his games.

The playground is a mucky mess,
Blood all over the floor,
From the fight that occurred this morning,
By the playtime door.

The bully is now happy,
To see what he has done,
To the child that's limping,
Now it's all gone.

Rebecca Croft (11)
Manston Primary School

Classroom War

Trapped, under lock and key,
'I'll be back in a minute,'
Screeched the teacher, 'and then you'll be free.'

Locked the door slowly,
A large cheer heard,
'Come on, let's play some football,
Or rugby with the school gerbil.'

Paint flying, a battlefield of messy mayhem,
Chaos all around,
Until the teacher rolls back in,
Detention you'll all understand.

Liam Berry (11)
Manston Primary School

Sarah's Scared

(Inspired by poem by Richard Edwards)

Sarah's scared of things at school,
Sarah's scared of the first day of school,
Scared of her brother's dark, dim room,
Scared of the bully that will come very soon.

Sarah's scared of things at school,
Sarah's scared of the dark corridor room,
Scared of the loudness in the air,
Scared of the bullies crowding round her now.

Sarah's scared of things at school,
Sarah's scared of the bullies punching her,
Scared of the blood dripping down her face,
Scared of the person who sent her here.

Sarah's scared of things at school,
Sarah's scared of the laughing behind her,
Scared of the bully's very big gang,
Scared of the bully that is really very cruel.

Victoria Scholes (11)
Manston Primary School

The Living Things At Playtime

I wonder if when it was playtime,
All of the pens and pencils ran about like little athletes,
With pens like surfers, riding rubbers as surfboards
In the teachers' cups of coffee
And rulers flying paper aeroplanes,
Pencil sharpeners voyage around the side of the pencil pot,
Like Evel Kenievel on his motorbike,
Going around the wall of death,
Each one of them scramble as they hear the whistle blow
And a stampede of feet thundering the ground,
Bumping into each other, they hurry back to the basket.

Jake Bleasby (10)
Manston Primary School

My Fierce Anger

My eyes are red-hot
My head is about to blow, it is flaming hot
Fire running through my veins
My stomach bubbling inside

My. . . mum . . .

Blood running out of my eyes
I am about to blow
My heart pounding like mad

Took . . . my . . .

I am punching the floor
My legs burning, ready to kick out
Now my veins are snapping like mad
I can't stop it

. . . Gamecube.

Jack Young (9)
Manston St James CE Primary School

Caterpillar Bye-Bye

Creepy crawling caterpillar
Slivers through the wet shiny grass
Up onto a leaf he goes, caterpillar. Bye-bye.

The children come out to play
And caterpillar goes away
When the children go in
Caterpillar comes out.

Natalie Wainman (8)
Manston St James CE Primary School

Burning Anger!

My face, red as fire
My feet, black as coal
My eyes, sizzling like burning sausages
Because

My sister . . .

My mouth breathing like a charging bull
My anger, red as sudden danger
My nose, bleeding black fire

Called me . . .

My anger, ready to fire out of my feet
I think I am going to blow up
And then I do

. . . Black tooth!

Laura Weed (9)
Manston St James CE Primary School

Dogs

Dogs are cute
Dogs are funny
Dogs are fast
Dogs go in races and shows
Dogs go to the vets
Dogs go to the kennels
Dogs are so cute and funny
Because they bump into things
Dogs are cute
Dogs are funny
Dogs are fast.

Abigail Moss (7)
Manston St James CE Primary School

My Anger

My anger, red as fire
My eyes turning to coal
My breath turning into a gale force wind

Because

My favourite . . .

Some nasty boys came
They tried to nick it
But then blew it up

Car . . .

I was so cross steam came out of my ears
I stamped so hard that
The car started to roll down the street

. . . Blew up!

Tomas Spink (9)
Manston St James CE Primary School

The Roller Coaster

It goes up and down and round and round
And of course it speeds left and right
Round the loop the loop it goes
Upside down the right way round!
But you must be warned that if it stops on the top of a loop
Then down you go!
Bang!
You're knocked out cold
You appear in hospital with a broken neck.

Jack McMaster (8)
Manston St James CE Primary School

My Eyes Red As Fire

My eyes, red as fire
My hair, red as blood
My nose snorts like a bull
My mouth, black and smoking

Because my baby cousin . . .

My belly bubbles like a kettle
I feel my body on fire
My heart as black as coal

Chewed . . .

My feet blazing
I am ready to go into space
My teeth black and red

. . . My favourite toy.

Natasha Round (8)
Manston St James CE Primary School

The Dinner Hall

Deep, down in the dinner hall
Clack, cold chips, mouldy meatballs
Chatting children, tired teachers, mess
Mess, mess, squished sandwiches
Melted munches dancing dinner ladies
All down in the dinner hall

Alycia Rose Milner (10)
Manston St James CE Primary School

Jack Called Me Fatty

My eyes, sizzling
My hair, black like ash
My head getting ready to explode
Like dynamite
Because:
                    Jack . . .

My blood, steaming
My head is like a storm
My mouth boils
Like a volcano
                    Called me . . .

My fists are ready to punch
My feet are ready to kick him
My stomach is going in and out
Like a hurricane
                    . . . Fatty!

Hayden Pride (9)
Manston St James CE Primary School

Tiger

T iger, tiger look at the tiger
I t is hiding behind the tree
G etting angry, now it's roaring
E dging nearer and nearer to us
R un, run as fast as you can.

James Sanderson (8)
Manston St James CE Primary School

My Dad Ducked Me In The Pool

I feel like a ball of fire
My face, like lots of nails digging me
My hair as dirty as coal
My mouth, like as if I've had my mouth ripped off
Because:

My dad . . .

Rocks falling from the sky
Thunderstorm and lightning crash straight down killing everybody in
the pool.

Ducked me . . .

My heart getting ripped out of my ribcage
Red blood falls from my eyes, my dad screaming
As he gets killed.

. . . In the pool!

Jack Nelmes (9)
Manston St James CE Primary School

My Football Poem

I love to kick my football around the yard
It's not easy, it's not hard
Football is special and takes a lot of skill
When I score a goal, I get a real thrill
I get near to the goal, I take aim
Wow I've scored, we've won the game!

Thomas Fisher (8)
Manston St James CE Primary School

Rabbit

See those rabbits hopping on the ground
Going up, up, up and down
They are cute little animals and quite small
Just watch out for the rabbit next door.

Natalie Austin (8)
Manston St James CE Primary School

I'm Angry!

I'm scorching, black as coal
My eyes are as red as fire
My fists are boiling hot
My head's exploding like a thundering roar
Because:

My brother . . .

My stomach burning like a torpedo
My heart is pounding like a blizzard
My mouth is breathing like an earthquake.

Threw me . . .

My hair is as hot as boiling fire
My nose is as black as the night
I think I'll turn into the Hulk
My nostrils are breathing fire.

. . . On the floor!

Seb Marsh (9)
Manston St James CE Primary School

Hope

Hope is a smooth sea-blue
It tastes like a sweet fruitcake
It smells like an ocean perfume
It sounds like a smooth, echoing sound
Hope lives in the bottom of my heart.

Abigail Heraty (9)
Manston St James CE Primary School

My Eyes Roaring Like Thunder

My stomach bubbling like a volcano
My eyes like sizzling sausages
My hair like hailstones
When I breathe, it's like a typhoon
Because:

My brother!

My heart's beating like a wrecking ball
I stamp my foot like an earthquake
I feel like I'm a giant

Took my!

I think I'm going to boil over
My fist like a rock
My mouth spilling out fire
My nose like lightning

PS2 games!

Jason Moore (9)
Manston St James CE Primary School

Rabbits

I love rabbits
They hop around
On the ground
In the summer
They're in their run
Having fun
I love rabbits
They hop up and down
And make no sound.

Amelia Scott (7)
Manston St James CE Primary School

My Roaring Anger!

My hair, sticking up like spikes on a cactus
My face, red as a dragon's tail
My blood boiling hot, as rage!
Because:

My sister . . .

Lightning running through my veins
Thunder crashing and clattering
Hailstones bursting out of the clouds
Hurricane roaring through the winds

Took my . . .

Hearing, yelling and shouting through my
Ears I can't help it.
Fire burning
My heart pounding like water pumping
Gameboy!

Danielle Manning (8)
Manston St James CE Primary School

Burning Anger!

My hair, black as the night
My eyes, dark as blazing fire
My nose breathes hot fire
Because:

My mum let . . .

My mouth breathes out dark words
I stamp my feet like I am squeezing
All the blood out of me

My cat out . . .

I scream like a gale and the wind whistling
My heart, pounding like flames of fire
My nostrils, bubbling like a kettle.

. . . And it got run over!

Harriet Laverick (9)
Manston St James CE Primary School

My Brother Threw A Book At Me

I'm angry!
It was an accident
And then he did it
Because:

My brother . . .

My mouth, breathing fire out like a boiling kettle.
My eyes pop out like a sizzling pan
My hair, black as dirty coal with anger inside me.

Threw a book . . .

My eyes, whistling like a train on a track
My heart, racing like a red bull
My head, feels like it will fall off.

. . . At me.

Molly Jones (9)
Manston St James CE Primary School

The Steaming Anger

My throat is burning like an angry lion
My eyes are steaming like a volcano
My hair is black, dark coal.
Because:

My best friend . . .

My hair is like a volcano exploding
My heart is burning in a pan
My heart, pounding like fire.

Stole my turn . . .

I can break a storm
My heart is like a sizzling pan
Then I explode!

. . . On the computer.

Lauren Huddlestone (8)
Manston St James CE Primary School

When I'm Angry

I see red
My hair goes hot and starts to burn
A storm whizzing round the room
Because:

My mum . . .

My stomach feels like a storm
My eyes bubbling like mad
My hand so near exploding
My head swirling like a blizzard.

Woke . . .

I am bubbling like mad
The whizzing starts slowing down
I yell.

. . . Me up!

Harriet Darcy (9)
Manston St James CE Primary School

My Anger!

Breath as hot as fire
My tongue on fire
I can't believe it
Aarrgghh, need water.

My motorbike . . .

Help, I need help quick
I'm about to blow up
Aarrgghh, need medicine for my headache.

Is out of . . .

What shall I do?
Noooo, help! Need fire extinguisher for my anger
I'm on fire, aarrgghh!

. . . Petrol!

Alexander Crosbie-Wright (8)
Manston St James CE Primary School

Blazing Mad

My eyes, red as fire, blazing like lava
I feel like I can bend steel
I could explode into space
I feel like I am about to set on fire.
Because:

My dog . . .

I think I'll turn into the Hulk and rip apart my house and run away
I feel like I could rip my face off
My blood, hot as volcano lava, could come out of my head.

Bit my . . .

It could burn the sky and clouds
I feel like I could smash all the walls
A tsunami could come with a typhoon
Thunder and lightning all over.

. . . Hand!

Dominic Evans (8)
Manston St James CE Primary School

Brenda The Blender

Brenda the blender cuts and hacks at all the condemned food
She's in a mood, getting faster and faster
The hum of her blades is getting louder and higher
Until she is like an opera singer
Whizzing and whining like a Catherine wheel
The food is turning to a thick pulp
Then suddenly her power's turned off
She goes into a deep drowsy sleep
Until she is needed again.

Andrew Battye (11)
Manston St James CE Primary School

My Bad Anger!

My eyes are black, as stormy night
My face red, as sizzling bacon and egg
My hair frizzy, like a lightning storm
My face bursting out with flames
Because:

                    My brother . . .

My hair is on fire
My body is red and blue
My heart pounding so fast
My heart roaring like it's never roared before

                    Messed . . .

My hair is like an afro
The earth is going to burst.

                    My room up!

Kia Clinton-Muncey (8)
Manston St James CE Primary School

Running A Race - Cinquain

Huff, puff
Run away fast
Oh quick, he's catching me
Look . . . I can see the finish line
Made it!

Laura Dixon (11)
Manston St James CE Primary School

Blazing Anger

My hair red as fire, steaming like a volcano
My eyes black and rusty
My hands exploding with fire
My heart pounding like a world of anger
Because:

                    My brother . . .

So angry, I could lift a house
So angry, I could blast into space
All tornados destroying the city
So angry, my voice like a thunderstorm.

                    Wouldn't let me play . . .

I feel like I could bend a piece of steel
I feel like I could punch a skyscraper down
I feel like I could rip a house down.

                    On my *own* Playstation 2!

Luke Cheetham (9)
Manston St James CE Primary School

Mr Rumble

Mr Rumble the earthquake gets angry
And starts to shake with frustration
Then cracks
And takes no prisoners
As he wobbles the ground and pulls down the buildings
He sucks the cars down his mouth
And taunts people by following them
Then *boom*, he pushes two cars into each other
They blow up
After this he cools down and decides he's done enough for one day
But he'll be back, he roars
And when he is, he won't hold back!

Ashley Walls (11)
Manston St James CE Primary School

My Hair As Red As Fire

My hair as red as fire
My fists as black as coal
My heart beating so fast it could burst.

Louis called . . .

My mouth, breathing like a gale
My head sizzles like fried toast
My eyes so red they could pop out.

Me . . .

Blazing anger
I feel like I want to kill Louis
I feel like a hurricane
My roar is as loud as a tiger.

. . . Coconut.

Kristan-lewis Bratton (9)
Manston St James CE Primary School

A Twister

The destroyer
It starts up life, small like a baby
It grows by feeding off the land
The destroyer destroys everything in its path
It takes people's homes
The spinning thing spins round like a dancer
It quickly moves round from place to place
Soon the destroyer comes back to where it's started
Spitting out all the things it's destroyed and collected
It soon gets dizzy, like someone playing dizzy dollies
Goes back to the waters and sleeps as long as it wants.

Ashley Hullock (11)
Manston St James CE Primary School

Sizzling Hot Fire

My hair sizzling like a hot frying pan
My roar as loud as a stampede
My eyes glowing like a red hot fire
My head thumping so hard that it could burst
Because

My cousin . . .

My stomach bubbling like a steaming hot kettle
My face burning like a boiling fire
My ears explode like a steam train smoking
My nose breathing like a thunderstorm

Broke my . . .

My hands ready to punch
My heart beating so hard that it could pop out
My blood turning black

Play station!

Dean Bland (9)
Manston St James CE Primary School

Bonfire Night

I love bonfires
I like the way they crackle
I love the colours
I like the way bonfires keep you nice and warm!

Then the fireworks!
I love the Roman candles
I like the big display rockets
And best of all the colours they make!

And best of all the food
All the gorgeous toffee apples
And the pork pies
Maybe even hot dogs.

Charles Dunkley (11)
Manston St James CE Primary School

My Heart As Hot As Fire

My heart, pumping like mad
My eyes as hot as fire
My face, going very, very red!
My ears, bursting with steam!
Because:

                         My sister. . .

My blood as hot as a kettle boiled one hundred million times!
My mouth breathing fire and exploding lava!
Volcanoes erupting everywhere you look!

                    Dropped a mattress . . .

My hair, roasting like fire!
My hair, ready to burst out flames
My fist, ready to punch!
My hair, steaming like lava!

                        . . . On my head.

Shaun Binns (9)
Manston St James CE Primary School

Being Vicious!

I see red; my ears have boiling, sizzling steam
My hair with black coal
My fists with giant flames
My breath like a blizzard

                         My mum didn't let me . . .

I turn into the Incredible Hulk
My face turns green
I rip my boxers off and my t-shirt
My muscles turns as big as volcanoes

                         Watch my favourite . . .

The Earth explodes
My eyes go as red as fire

                    . . . T.V. programme!

Azrael Bell (9)
Manston St James CE Primary School

Moaning Molly

My Molly's a marvellous moaner
She moans for a month at a time
She makes our home life a misery
That moaning Molly of mine

She moans about me in the mornings
She moans to my dad who's called Mike
She moans to my mum who's a medic
She moans with all of her might

It's mushrooms that make her most mardy
And maggots and mice make her mad
She's mastered all methods of moaning
Her miserable moods make me sad

Maybe my Molly might mellow
Her moaning make way for more mirth
The message for my moaning Molly
Is that misery and moods have no worth

Although my Molly's a moaner
Her mind has been marvellously made
Give her music, marshmallows and make-up
And her masterly moaning might fade!

Jack Wildsmith (10)
Manston St James CE Primary School

The Eighth Dress

Dear Grandad
Thanks for the dress
I'll wear it later
Bright pink is my favourite
That's the eighth dress you've bought me
Anyway thank you

Laura Place (10)
Manston St James CE Primary School

Twister Moves

Twister moves
Gives you a little groove
Twister moves
Working like horses' hooves

Twister moves
Choose a coloured mat
Twister moves
Choose a funky track

Twister moves
Teaching you how to dance
Twister moves
You need to use your hands

Twister moves
Listen to the music
Twister moves
You might overdo it

Twister moves
A brilliant game
Twister moves
My friends think the same.

Sophie Jagger (10)
Manston St James CE Primary School

There Was An Old Man Of Leeds

There was an old man of Leeds
His job was killing weeds
He saw Sol Campbell
And fell on a bramble
That distressing old man of Leeds

Alfie Leeds (11)
Manston St James CE Primary School

Him

I look at him
But no words are spoken
I dream of him
But those dreams don't come true
I am funny around him
But the sound of laughter is not heard
I try to act cool
But it ends up in a phase of humiliation
I smile at him
But that smile is not returned
One day I kissed him in the spur of the moment
And it all ended in tears.

Jenny Tootell (10)
Manston St James CE Primary School

The Camp

It creeps
On a dark night
Something moving slowly
Something unzipping my green tent
It strikes . . .

Rosie Allen (10)
Manston St James CE Primary School

The Sun - Cinquain

The sun
Yellow and bright
People are having fun
Then the clouds come and make it dull
Coats on!

Rachel Clark (11)
Manston St James CE Primary School

The Crazy, Cosy Cottage

In the bathroom
There is
A bath filled with mouldy brown water
A glass at the end of the bath with green and black mouldy teeth in it
Three giant spiders living under the seat of the toilet
A sink filled with slimy, smelly soap
A broken window with whistling wind coming through
A smashed, broken light bulb with scattered glass on the floor
And a bird nesting in the shower.

Rebecca Gibbs (11)
Manston St James CE Primary School

The Crazy, Cosy Cottage

In the dining room
There is
A pair of ladders
A large tub of paint
A sofa covered in an old sheet
10 white roses in a crystal vase
A roller in a paint tray
A white, wet washed wall
And my dad in scruffy clothes covered in paint.

Emma Sutcliffe (10)
Manston St James CE Primary School

Big Feet

There once was a man with big feet
Who had the urge to eat
He ate up a pie in the blink of an eye
Then couldn't get out of his seat.

Dylan Parr (10)
Manston St James CE Primary School

Fireworks

Zooming, whirling, spinning round
Fireworks showering from the sky
Orange sparks, blue showers
Flying high, then crashing back
Pink and purple splashing down
Pie and peas, jacket potatoes with cheese
Gingerbread men and doorstep bread
Yummy, yummy, yum
Bang, bang, wow, cool
Babies scream, children shout
Dogs howl, cats cry
Grown-ups yell and moan
With fireworks cascading everywhere
Bonfire Night's great, but stay safe
And do *not* get hurt!

Emma Gelley (11)
Manston St James CE Primary School

The Staffroom

So close yet so far away
So distant and forbidden
Where teachers actually have fun
And laugh and giggle
All through playtime!

It must be a wonderful place
With fridges full of chocolate and pop
And PlayStation 2s plugged into five plasma screens
Well it has to be, if they miss it so much, that they're grumpy
All through lesson time!

Adam Kerrigan (11)
Manston St James CE Primary School

Sir Winter

I hear Sir Winter coming
He crawls out of his bed
All the children are playing
With a woolly hat on their head

I'm going to go and freeze the lakes
And cover the grass with white
Everyone will bring their skates
And they'll be such a sight

Sir Winter has an ice-cold nose
And always wears his hat
He has icicles instead of toes
And he's very, very fat.

Jennifer Dunwell (10)
Manston St James CE Primary School

Dog Fear

Bang! Bang! That's all I hear
It's round about the same time of year
These big things bang in the sky
Other ones squeal and cry

All the noises that I hear
Make me run away in fear
Some are red, green and blue
They shower down, before I knew

Bang! Bang! That's all I hear
I wish this noise would disappear
And *not* come back the following year!

Jennifer Roberts (11)
Manston St James CE Primary School

5th November

Get the cats and dogs indoors
Grab the fireworks out of the drawers
Set them out for a wacky display
Boom, boom, hip, hip, hooray

Showers of pink, purple and blue
Dancing in the sky, just for you
Get the sparklers out for the kids
Boom, crackle, crackle, whiz

The bonfire's flickering up so high
Glorious patterns hitting the sky
Children's faces all aglow
Bonfire Night, they love it so

There's toffee apples and hot dogs to eat
Lots of friends for you to meet
Rockets and Catherine wheels for all to see
Lots of treats for you and me

One firework left and off it goes
Now the party must draw to a close
Flames burning low as we say goodbye
Remembering rockets high in the sky.

Chelsea Shepherd (11)
Manston St James CE Primary School

There's A Little Old Man From Leeds

There's a little old man from Leeds
Who swallowed a packet of seeds
He fell over a chair
And lost his underwear
That silly old man from Leeds.

Jessica Nolan (11)
Manston St James CE Primary School

What I Will Miss Most

The things that are in this list
Is what I'll miss most from school
When I'm at school I'll never use my fist
And I definitely won't use it as a tool

I will miss my friends so much
Even though we will still keep in touch
I will miss all of the teachers
And will miss all the school features

I won't worry though I'll visit some time
And I may even bring the teacher a bottle of wine
I'll miss everyone still
But I won't bring money in a till

I've got one more thing to say to you all
I'll miss you all if you're big or small.

Alice Lane (11)
Manston St James CE Primary School

Fireworks

Booming, banging, filling the sky
Round the Catherine wheel goes
The rockets go up and *bang!* They burst before your eyes
The bonfire's crackling, bursting with flames
Off goes a fountain with sparkling rain
The bonfire's big, making lots of heat
A Roman candle's starting, 'Look!' *Bang, bang, bang*
Red, yellow, green and blue and who invented these, who oh who?

Thomas Appleyard (10)
Manston St James CE Primary School

My Little Friend

I have a little friend
He's not a fish
But does eat out of a dish
He has brown fur
He's not a cat
He doesn't purr
He's small and cute
Sometimes lives in my boot
He has a pointy nose
And little pink toes
He loves to nibble cheese
His name is Hercules.

Elliot Walls (11)
Manston St James CE Primary School

In The Cellar

In the cellar
There is
A creaking, clanking, chattering box
97 mimicking cockroaches
A leaking toilet pipe
A manky smelly sock
A wet, buttonless bear
A bouncing trampoline
And a dead-beaten, teeth-marked mouse!

Leigh Towse (11)
Manston St James CE Primary School

The Whirlpool

The whirlpool spins fast and furious
Grabbing and gobbling everything in his way
Twisting and turning, the mad thing whizzes around the ocean bed
He is extremely strong
And finally disappears
And all that is left is a fish bone.

Amy Wood (10)
Manston St James CE Primary School

Why Not? - Cinquain

Why not?
Inspiration
As I write I have none
I can't think of any cinquains
Just, why?

Mathew Kerry (10)
Manston St James CE Primary School

A Funny Old Man Called Bill

A funny old man called Bill
Lived at the top of a hill
He now lives in Leeds
A house full of weeds
What a strange old man called Bill.

Lucy Packman (11)
Manston St James CE Primary School

Winter

Winter is cold
Winter is snowy
Winter is calm
Winter is frosty

Winter brings joy
Winter brings Christmas
Winter brings presents
Winter brings love.

Megan Boldison (11)
Manston St James CE Primary School

Tsunami - Cinquain

Boom! Crash!
The tidal wave
Hit . . . people dead, houses
Gone. Lives destroyed. Swept away. All
Cleared up.

Lauren Heraty (11)
Manston St James CE Primary School

Green

A meadow, fresh and light,
A lonely leaf, floating from a tall tree,
A cold mint-chip ice cream,
The warble of a thrush,
A light leading us on,
And an envious grin.

Emily Thomson (10)
Moorfield School

Dreams

I would like to hear the stars shooting
Through the air and make them into a necklace.
Capture the midnight sky and put it in my pocket.
Taste the melody of the sun and let it melt on my tongue
And smell the scent of sweet scones to share with everybody
I would like to drink all the dreams and make them come true
Live in a magical world and build a house out of rainbows
And watch fairies dance and I would join in . . .

Emma Goodwin-Jones (10)
Moorfield School

I Would Love To . . .

I would love to bottle up the cuddles with my cousin
To hold onto him when he grabs my finger and clings to me
I would love to sip my pride when I've done something spectacular
Capture the wind howling all around me on a cold winter's night
I would love to paint a picture of my feelings in an array of colours
And catch a snowflake to keep in a box
If only I could capture peace and eliminate hatred and war.

Lauren Richardson (11)
Moorfield School

Grey

Slow and wilting, it is tired and cruel
Droopy and desperate like a prisoner in a cell
Like being trapped in an iron cage I cannot escape from it
It swallows up all your happiness
Stuck inside with a storm cloud all around me
It is sad and dull and will suck you in.

Emily Layton (11)
Moorfield School

My Psalm Of Despair

Dear Lord,
Our hearts are filled with sorrow and despair,
My children are lost
In the dark death.

Lord,
Your love for me is like a candle,
Flickering, but never dying,
But Lord, why do you slay me,
With such misfortune?

Lord,
I am lost
No chinks of light appear
All because of the great wave.

Lord,
There is a famine and shortages of clean water
We are dying, gone, starving
None of the disaster can disappear.

Lord,
If you can hear me
Smite the wrong
Please Lord,
For my heart's sake
I'm bleeding with emotion
Please Lord,
Amen.

Georgie Henley (9)
Moorfield School

White Invader

Snow on trees like a patchwork blanket
White invader
Strangling flowers
Destroying colours
Starving animals
Cruel and thoughtless
Laughing at chaos
Smothering hedges
Trespassing on gardens
Giving secrets away
(Footprints of animals at night)
Arrives uninvited
Attacking the grass
Beginning to die
Slipping away quietly
Disappearing into the ground
And slithering down the drain
The trees cry with happiness
The garden shines with colour once again.

Bethan Daykin (9)
Moorfield School

Winter Weather

Snow flurries like dancing fairies in the night sky
Snow settling like crispy meringues
Stepping on crunchy ice like sugar cubes
Frost delicate like a ballerina
Ice like a cold shimmering mirror
Frost covers the grass like sherbet.

Emily Wood (8)
Moorfield School

Darkness

Darkness comes
   With owls hooting
Darkness comes
   With Dad snoring
Darkness comes
   With foxes snapping
Darkness comes
   With children screaming
Darkness comes
   With doors slamming
Darkness comes
   With dogs barking
Darkness comes
   With bushes rustling
Darkness comes
   With people shaking.

Rosie Phillip (7)
Moorfield School

My Winter Poem

Snow as fluffy as candyfloss
And bitter like a lemon
Ice, hard like a window
And sparkly like a crystal
Frost, chilly and ice-capped
Jack Frost painting the rooftops silver.

Emma Tankard (8)
Moorfield School

Darkness

Darkness comes
    With owls hooting
Darkness comes
    With foxes growling
Darkness comes
    With wolves howling
Darkness comes
    With mice squeaking
Darkness comes
    With dogs barking
Darkness comes
    With bats clicking
Darkness comes
    With frogs croaking
Darkness comes
    For bedtime.

Enya-Medi Wentling (7)
Moorfield School

Winter Poem

Snow like a giant white blanket
Ice as shiny as diamonds
And frost cruel and crispy
Like a sprinkle of icing sugar
The land covered in pure white
Skidding on glittering ice
Jack Frost leaping from roof to roof
Turning them white.

Laura Layton (8)
Moorfield School

Darkness

Darkness comes
        With owls hooting
Darkness comes
        With Dad snoring
Darkness comes
        With floorboards creaking
Darkness comes
        With wolves howling
Darkness comes
        With clock ticking
Darkness comes
        With babies crying
Darkness comes
        With bins clattering
Darkness comes
        It's time for bed.

Ellie-Mai Driver (6)
Moorfield School

Abigail

A bigail is my name
B lue eyes I have
I   have a sister called Chessie
G eorge is my brother
A nnabelle is my favourite toy
I   love sweets
L ovely the world I live in.

Abigail Stott (7)
Moorfield School

How I Wonder . . .

Why do dewdrops glisten?
They steal it from the stars.

How does mist move?
It hitches a ride on the wind.

When do streams giggle?
When they play leapfrog with the stones.

What is a pot of gold?
The colours of the rainbow.

Where does the wind sleep?
In the boughs of trees and creaky doors.

Who is the noise?
Sound itself . . .

Stephanie Ford (10)
Moorfield School

Darkness

Darkness comes
With my dog barking
Darkness comes
With owls hooting
Darkness comes
With mice scampering
Darkness comes
With doors slamming
Darkness comes
With trees swishing
Darkness comes
With wind whistling
Darkness comes
With me going to bed.

Millie Clapham (6)
Moorfield School

Winter

When does the wind celebrate?
As the wrapping paper dissolves.

Where does the snow sleep?
On a four-poster cloud.

What does the morning mist eat for breakfast?
A dewdrop from a silver birch in the cornfields.

Who talks to the cold, weeping willow when he's sad?
His old fellow frosted leaves all lying on the ground.

How does the icy grass feel when he's cold on the ground?
He feels lonely until summer arrives.

Amy Bolser (10)
Moorfield School

Wishes

I would like to take home
The reflection of the moon shimmering on rippling water
Cuddle the joy of lambs in spring
Prancing and leaping about
Capture the feeling of cuddling a kitten by the fire
On a winter's night
Sip the mist wafting mysteriously off the grass
On a frosty morning.

If I could bottle all this up inside
I would never feel sad or lonely again.

Sophie Stone (10)
Moorfield School

It Was So Quiet That . . .

It was so quiet that,
I could hear my eyelids drooping
It was so quiet that,
I could hear a ladybird snoring.
It was so quiet that,
I could hear planets spinning like a roundabout
It was so quiet that,
I could hear the stars shimmering far beyond.
It was so quiet that,
I could hear sunbeams shining on the dewy flowers.
It was so quiet that,
I could hear the clouds floating along lazily
It was so quiet that,
I could hear buds opening slowly
It was so quiet that,
I could hear a blade of grass dancing in the summer's breeze.

Emma Dracup (9)
Moorfield School

Wishes

I would like to see the whistling of the wind
When the night falls,
To hear blackberries ripen
As they burst with juice,
To taste a warm summer's evening
When sweetness fills the air,
To smell the droplets of the sun
As roses and jasmine bloom.
I would like to touch someone's happiness
And trap it forever.

Martha Crossley (10)
Moorfield School

Private, Peaceful

It was so calm I could see
A blade of grass grumble and groan
Under the weight of the powerful wind . . .

It was so silent I could sense
Clouds floating across the
Velvet sky . . .

It was so peaceful I could pick up
The gentle beat of a caterpillar's heartbeat
As it crawls along a ledge . . .

It was so gentle I could hear
Birds' wings flap like
Flying on a kite . . .

It was so quiet I could hear
The planet roll over
In its icy sleep.

Bryony Skinn (9)
Moorfield School

A Whisper In A Poem

It was so silent I could hear the heat
Rising from the roasting fire.

It was so still I could hear the birds' wings
Scraping the clouds.

It was so calm I could hear the ants
Scurrying about like busy housewives.

It was so quiet I could feel the blood
Running in my veins.

It was so silent I could hear the glue
Drying up like sausages sizzling in a pan.

I was so small I could hear everything.

Emma Tapper (9)
Moorfield School

Best Friends

Would a best friend
Scream at you loudly
For no reason?
Mine did.
And would a best friend
Creep up behind you
Like a mysterious panther?
Mine did.

Would a best friend
Cheer you on
When you're in
Last place?
Mine did.
And would a best friend
Include you in every game?
Mine did.

Would a best friend
Say, 'That's OK, let's
Forgive and forget?'
I did.

John Best (8)
North Featherstone J&I School

Secrets

I love secrets when they belong to me
My friends gather round me, staring
I won't tell, because I am a tease!

I love secrets when they belong to Mum
Her eyes tell me she's hiding something
But she won't tell me what!

I hate secrets when they belong to my sister
She stays silent and won't say a word
How ignorant!

Victoria Rennison (9)
North Featherstone J&I School

Friendship

Would a best friend creep up on you
Push you and shout in your ear
Because he was jealous . . . ?
    Mine did.

Would a best friend not let you
Be on their side at football and leave you out . . . ?
    Mine did

Would a best friend frantically run up to you
Say hello, happily laugh with you
And share their sweets . . . ?
    Mine did.

Would a best friend say sorry for leaving you
Out at football and for not letting you be on
Their team . . . ?
    Mine did.

And would you say simply, 'That's OK,
Never mind . . .'
    I did.

Joe Roberts (9)
North Featherstone J&I School

Secrets

I hate secrets when they belong to Mum
When I ask, 'Have you got any secrets?' she just trots away
How annoying!

I hate secrets when they belong to Dad
When you say a sentence with the word 'secret' in,
He just changes the subject.
How boring!

I hate secrets when they belong to my sister
She creeps and hides away till I'm gone
How sly!

Ethan Vickers (9)
North Featherstone J&I School

Friendship

Would a best friend . . .
Cheat on you for no reason,
Shout in front of your face
Steal a precious ring that isn't theirs?
        Mine did.

Would a best friend . . .
Help you when you're hurt
Turn up at your house and invite you for tea,
Buy you a magnificent gift?
        Mine did.

Play with you in the school playground,
Ring you up and say that she's very sorry like a true friend would
Buy a best friend card for you
Play with you like a true and faithful friend
        And try to be gentle and kind?

        Is your friend a true friend?
            Mine is.

Katie Morgan (8)
North Featherstone J&I School

Secrets

I love secrets when they belong to me
They are so special I write them in my diary,
Oh! Happy secrets!

I love secrets when they belong to Mum
They sparkle in her eyes, very shiny
Secrets are wonderful!

But I hate secrets when they are about me
Because everyone sniggers and starts to be selfish
Who else wants to make me cry?

Meg Nowell (7)
North Featherstone J&I School

Best Friends

Has your best friend got as much energy as a Springer Spaniel?
Mine has.
Has your best friend got twinkle toes like a ballerina?
Mine has.
Has your best friend got the leap of a panther?
Mine has.

Has your best friend got a strange sense of humour?
Mine hasn't.
Has you best friend stomped their feet like an elephant?
Mine hasn't.
Has your best friend got a miserable walk like a tortoise?
Mine hasn't.

My best friend is perfect, because she is the best in the world.

Abigail Ziemniak (9)
North Featherstone J&I School

Secrets

I hate secrets when they belong to my mum . . .
She calls me over then says, 'I should not tell you, because
A secret is a secret.' It drives me mad!

I love secrets when they belong to my sister . . .
Because she is the only one who tells me everything
How kind!

I love secrets when they belong to my dad . . .
Because he wants to tell me, but he can't, so he always
Changes the subject. It's hilarious!

Ella Gibbs (8)
North Featherstone J&I School

Best Friends

Would a best friend meanly talk behind your back,
Take something that is yours without telling you?
      Mine did.

Would a best friend leave you out and play
With other children, blame you cruelly for what they've done?
      Mine did.

Would a best friend come to you, give you what she took
And say sorry?
      Mine did.

Would a best friend kindly help you
When you have hurt yourself?
      Mine did.

And would a best friend whisper in your ear
And say,
'I'm sorry, can we be friends?'
      Mine did.

Melissa Guest (9)
North Featherstone J&I School

Friendship

Would a best friend climb up his cage wall to reach you?
Would a best friend bite your finger?
Would a best friend jump into your arms?
Mine did.
Would a best friend dance to music?
Would a best friend run like a cheetah?
Would a best friend break out of his cage and jump into your shoe?
My friend is a terrific, trusting pet.
My friend is a terrific hamster.

Scott Lapish (8)
North Featherstone J&I School

Best Friends

Would a best friend . . .
Take over your favourite game
And run away with your shoe?
>Mine did.

Would a best friend . . .
Shout in your face
And pick on you wherever you are?
>Mine did.

Would a best friend . . .
Say pick your favourite game
And give your new shoe back?
>Mine did.

Would a best friend . . .
Say sorry for shouting in your face
And sorry for picking on you?
>Mine did.

And would a best friend . . .
Say, 'It's OK
I forgive you.'
>I did.

Adam Nix (9)
North Featherstone J&I School

Secrets

I hate secrets when they belong to friends
They always whisper and sneak away and
Then snigger at me. How sly!

I love secrets when they belong to Mum
Her eyes tell she is hiding something special,
But won't say what.

I love secrets when they belong to Dad
He always calls me over and pretends he's forgotten,
What a tease!

Katie Crawshaw (9)
North Featherstone J&I School

Secrets

I love secrets when they belong to Dad,
He doesn't tell me for two days and then
Slowly says he's forgotten.
How sly!

I love secrets when they're whispered
But when they're not told I feel furious.
How awful!

But I hate secrets when they belong to friends,
When they belong to someone else
They sometimes make me cry.

Sarah Pashley (9)
North Featherstone J&I School

Secrets

I love secrets when they belong to my mum . . .
She calls me over, then says, 'No!'
How annoying!

I hate secrets when people keep them away from me
Run off whenever I come near them.

I love secrets when they belong to my best friend
Her eyes sparkle and glisten.

Samantha Still (9)
North Featherstone J&I School

Death

Death is black
It smells like a steaming kettle
Death tastes like cracking glass
It sounds like screaming and crying
It feels like you have lost your heart
Death lives in a scrapyard.

Grace Somerville (10)
Our Lady's Primary School

The Tsunami

Give these people a helping hand,
For what happened beneath the land.

The sea came up and made a big wave
Many lives we can help save.

Give these people a helping hand,
For what happened beneath the land.

In our school we raised some money
To make their lives not dark, but sunny.

Give these people a helping hand,
For what happened beneath the land.

Lots of houses washed away
Please will you help us pray?

Give these people a helping hand,
For what happened beneath the land.

Jessica Beaumont (8)
Our Lady's Primary School

Death

Death is black
It smells like rotten cabbage
Death tastes mouldy and gritty
It sounds like a bagpipe being played badly
It feels cold and lumpy
Death lives in the middle of a graveyard.

Natasha Griffiths (10)
Our Lady's Primary School

The Tsunami Song

Give these people a helping hand,
Let the children understand.

In our school, we helped them live,
Why don't you help the poor and give?

Give these people a helping hand,
Let the children understand.

Many children are crying today,
Let us take the pain away.

Give these people a helping hand,
Let the children understand.

Waves came up and washed the sand
So make more families understand.

Give these people a helping hand,
Let everyone understand.
        Please!

Elliott Wilkes (9)
Our Lady's Primary School

Old Age

Old age is grey
It smells like a rotten egg
Old age tastes like liver
It sounds like click, clock, crunch
It feels wrinkly and very old
Old age lives in the rocking chair.

Brad Cascarino (10)
Our Lady's Primary School

The Snow Dog Express

The sledge is pulled
By dogs fluffy and white,
Travelling across the North Pole,
Morning and night.

They only stop to eat
And quickly take a rest,
Then off they go again
Now they're heading west.

They're on their way home,
Back to the house of ice,
It may be very cold
But they think it's very nice.

Bobby Jones (8)
Our Lady's Primary School

Old Age

Old age is grey
It smells like raw fish
Old age tastes like sour lemons
It sounds like a creaking chair
It feels wrinkly and rough
Old age lives in a rocking chair.

Katie-Louise Smith (10)
Our Lady's Primary School

War

War is black
It smells like blood
War tastes like burnt meat
It sounds like nails on a blackboard
It feels like a gunshot
It lives in the heart of a bullet.

Marco Longoni (10)
Our Lady's Primary School

Hate

Hate is black and blue
It smells like dung on your shoe
It tastes like rotten tomatoes that are smelly
And it sounds like a baby crying in your belly
It feels like a rocky rock
And it lives in a cruel man's shop.

Thomas Hind (9)
Our Lady's Primary School

Old Age

Old age is grey
It smells like rotten apples
Old age tastes like bitter liver
It sounds like a creaking chair
It feels like soft and wrinkly
It lives in a rocking chair.

Tyler Vayro
Our Lady's Primary School

Hope

Hope is blue
Hope smells like flowers
Hope tastes like blueberries
Hope sounds peaceful
Hope feels smooth
Hope lives on a sunny beach.

Matthew Wild (9)
Our Lady's Primary School

Old Age

Old age is grey
It smells like rotten apples
Old age tastes like liver
It sounds like someone scrunching paper
It feels like wool and cotton
Old age lives in a rocking chair.

Lauren Clarke (9)
Our Lady's Primary School

War

The colour of war is red
War smells like burning rubber
War tastes like trickling water in your mouth
War sounds like catapults firing at walls
War feels like bricks falling on you!
War lives in the hearts of angry men.

Jonty Lendill (9)
Our Lady's Primary School

Hope

Hope is white
It smells like popcorn
Hope tastes like candyfloss
It sounds like a butterfly fluttering
Hope feels like the sun shining on you
Hope lives on a sunny beach.

Leah Gatenby (10)
Our Lady's Primary School

Death

Death is pitch-black
It smells of spilt blood
Death tastes like poison
It sounds like a gunshot
It feels like you're angry
It lives in a graveyard.

Matthew Gavaghan (9)
Our Lady's Primary School

Fear

Fear is black
Fear smells wet and horrid
It tastes like slugs
Fear is a scared and thudding sound
It feels like you're in pain
It lives right at the edge of your heart.

Holly Kneale McKeon (10)
Our Lady's Primary School

Death

Death is blood-red
It smells like a fire burning
Death tastes like poison
It sounds like a child screaming
It feels painful
Death lives in a graveyard.

Julianne Ruocco (10)
Our Lady's Primary School

Pain

Pain is black
It smells like burnt burgers
Pain tastes hot and spicy
It sounds like rocks clashing together
It feels hard and rough
Pain lives in a dark cave.

James Clark Dixon (9)
Our Lady's Primary School

Hate

Hate is brown
It smells like dirty pop
Hates tastes like dirty water
It sounds like screaming babies
It feels hard
Hate lives in a dark cave.

Courtney Gunby (9)
Our Lady's Primary School

War

War is grey
War smells like smoke
War tastes like blood
War sounds like guns shooting
War feels cold
War lives in smoke.

Liam Maddock (10)
Our Lady's Primary School

The Angry Cat

It climbs trees with his shocking sharp claws
When he gets up, there he'll hang
One day the trunk and branches
Will come falling down with a bang.

When it's night he lays in his basket
Don't disturb him or beware
He'll bite your legs and scratch your toes
And act like he doesn't care.

Josh Hooks (8)
Our Lady's Primary School

Hate

Hate is black
It smells like burning
It tastes like burnt chicken
Hate sounds like screaming
It feels like steam
Hate lives in a volcano.

Hayley Webster (9)
Our Lady's Primary School

Zombies

Zombies are eating creatures
They eat things all the time
They can be any shape or size,
And are covered all in slime.

Some have nails that are very long,
So be careful they don't scratch,
Although they're not so clever,
They're good at playing catch!

Ben O'Connell (8)
Our Lady's Primary School

About Me

My name is Jason
I am from Leeds
I sometimes climb up very big trees.

I ride my bike
From home to Josh's
Never fall in front of buses.

I like my house
My room is blue
But sometimes my sister makes my head
Go through the roof.

Jason Stevenson (9)
Our Lady's Primary School

Girls And Boys

Girls like flowers and playing with dolls,
They skip and dance all day long,
They play with hair and put make-up on,
They never like to do what's wrong.

Boys, however, can be naughty,
They like to play football,
And ride their bikes and jump in puddles,
And ignore the teacher's call.

Georgia Wade (8)
Our Lady's Primary School

My Secret Creature, Spike

I have a secret creature
He sits at the back of the class
He's sneaky and he's slimy
And his body is made of brass.

His hair is made of snakes
His fingers and toes are bent
His nose is long and pointed
And he lives in a blue tent.

He's been mine for two years now,
And nobody knows about him
My creature's name is Spike
He has a wife named Kim.

Nathan Sykes (8)
Our Lady's Primary School

My Pet Cat

Cats can be fat
Rats can be fine
But best of all, dogs can be both.
And mice can be small
And they can crawl
Dogs can be messy and scruffy.

Ryan Rowlands (9)
Our Lady's Primary School

My School

School is cool, school is great,
But sometimes I am really late!

My favourite has got to be maths
But I also enjoy the swimming baths.

My school has a computer suite
It's so exciting I can't stand the heat.

I'm also on the gymnastic team
If we win my face will beam.

My school is really the best
I would choose it out of all the rest.

Aaron Roberts (8)
Our Lady's Primary School

The Rapping Rat

Yo, yo, yo! I am the rapping rat,
I rap all day, I rap all night,
I am the rapping master
I rap until the morning light.

I like to wear sunglasses,
I have my eyebrow pierced,
I look like a gangster and
I am very fierce.

Joshua Padmore (8)
Our Lady's Primary School

My Friends

My friends are playful and kind
Better friends you'll never find

They are good at playing ball
And jumping towers very tall.

Without my friends I'd be really sad,
So with my friends I'm always glad.

Joshua Reed (8)
Our Lady's Primary School

My Bling, Bling Cat

I had a bling, bling cat
It saw a really fat rat
Near his bed on the mat.

Then my cat saw a dog
That was chasing after a frog
My bling, bling cat fell over a log!

Joe Harper (8)
Our Lady's Primary School

Summer

Summer!
Sometimes you get stung by bees,
And pretty flowers grow on trees
Time for children to fight with water
Better than winter when days are shorter!
Summer!

Daniel Phillips (9)
Our Lady's Primary School

Rugby Is Great!

R ugby is my favourite sport
U nion's my favourite type
'G oal,' they shout
B rave Leeds, Tykes on the run
Y ippee! They score

I would like to see them play
S uper rugby all the time

G reat!
R oss gets the kick
E ager for another try
A t Headingley Stadium
T ry! They score, the whistle goes and that ends the match.

Benjamin Kemp (7)
Richmond House School

People

I like to watch people passing by,
Flying in planes high up in the sky,
Walking, talking and riding a bike,
Running, jumping and taking a hike.
Fat, thin, short or tall,
Everyone likes to play football.
Hot or cold, wind or rain,
People rush past to catch the train.
I'm the girl in the wheelchair,
Who smiles, waves and brushes her hair.

Francesca Broadbridge-Kirbitson (7)
Richmond House School

My Hamster

Curled up in a ball now
Hammy's fast asleep
We're really, really happy
Because he's now ours to keep.

On Christmas morning
I rushed downstairs
To open all my gifts
And I saw an unusual shaped present.

What could it be?
As I ripped it open
I saw
Some tiny little pink things
They were tiny little paws!

It was Hammy!

Sam Sheehy (7)
Richmond House School

An Ogre

I heard a hairy ogre,
Who said he needed to do his morning yoga,
But he bumped his head on his bed.
The doctor said, 'Sleep in the shed,
And dye your hair red.'
He went purple with rage,
As he was due to go on stage.
He did not find this funny
So he went hopping mad like a bunny!

Lucas Smedley (7)
Richmond House School

One Orange Octopus

One orange octopus swimming in the sea,
Two thin tigers coming to meet me.

Three tiny tortoises all dressed in pink,
Four friendly flies waiting for a drink.

Five fat frogs leaping on the dock,
Six sweet sea lions sitting on a rock.

Seven smelly skunks sniffing about,
Eight enormous elephants with big snouts.

Nine naughty nightingales singing in the park,
Ten tiny termites eating in the dark.

Eleven elegant eagles flapping around,
Twelve terrified tigers strolling on the ground.

Thirteen tired turtles resting in bed,
Fourteen fried frogs fried by Fred.

Fifteen fed up fish eating lots more,
Sixteen sick snails laid by the door.

Seventeen slimy snakes slivering on a rock,
Eighteen electric eels trying to fix a lock.

Nineteen naughty nits hiding in hair,
Twenty terrifying tarantulas scaring the mare.

Charlotte Denison (10)
Richmond House School

Tag Rugby

Passing the ball from player to player
Scoring a try is the aim of the of game
Dropping the ball is definitely a shame
We tackle a player with the ball
Six tackles is the rule of the game.

Harrison Brown Raw (7)
Richmond House School

The Hippogriff's Beginning

The hippogriff's beginning . . .
For his wings he took the soaring falcons
The browns of the autumn
And the smoothness of the ice

For his legs he took the wild stallions
And the hooves of the untamed wildebeest
And the thrust of the wind

For his wrath he took Lord Zeus
And the rage of the mighty lion
And the flame of Erebus itself

For his beak he took the graceful eagles
For his eyes he took the moon and stars
And for his strike he took the crocodiles

And for his prey he took the unwary.

Henry Cranston (10)
Richmond House School

Colours

Colours, colours all around,
Look around your house,
What colours have you found?
Reds and yellows, green and blues I suppose.
Light may seem white to you,
But really it is a spectrum of all these colours.
Red, orange, yellow, green, blue, indigo and violet.
The world would be boring
If it was all grey.

Alex Barnett (7)
Richmond House School

One Lazy Lion

One lazy lion lurking loudly about.
Two stinging scorpions with big stinking snouts.

Three pounding pandas looking for some food.
Four hunky, hairy hens looking like a dude.

Five flirting fleas trying to find a fish.
Six slimy, slithering snakes have a dish.

Seven stinky skunks smelling everyone out.
Eight eating emus pecking peculiarly about.

Nine naughty nightingales singing in the wind.
Ten tiny tigers, their toys and trees have been binned.

Eleven enormous elephants in a saloon.
Twelve barnacle, bonkers baboons playing with balloons.

Thirteen tiring termites having fights.
Fourteen firing fleas looking at kites.

Fifteen cracking crocodiles eating on some kits.
Sixteen awful alligators wearing purple mitts.

Ashley Hemingway (11)
Richmond House School

Rugby's Great!

R ugby's great
U nion is the
G reatest type of rugby there is
B radford Bulls are the best
Y ippee! Yeah! They score
S uch a great sport

G reat to play
R oss gets the kick
E leven-six the score
A t Headingley Stadium
T he game is over and Leeds win.

Edward West (7)
Richmond House School

The Pig

It all began when Piggy was made.
She took the curliness of springs
And the springiness of pogo sticks
For her tail.

She took the pinkness of handbags
And the smell of sewers
For her looks.

She took the clippy-cloppy of high-heeled shoes
And the hardness of metal
For her hooves.

She took the greenness of grass
And the roundness of buttons
For her eyes.

She took the sharpness of claws
And the hardness of steel
For her teeth
And Piggy was made.

Eleanor Heffron (10)
Richmond House School

Ice And Snow

Ice, ice, frozen ice,
Ice, ice, cold ice,
My ice is starting to melt,
Ice, ice, wet ice,
Snow, snow, falling snow,
Snow, snow, falling on my head,
Snow, snow, melting snow.

Paul Millner (7)
Richmond House School

Hedgehogs

To make a hedgehog,
He took the pain from nettles,
He took the spikiness of sharks' teeth,
And made his spikes.

And for his eyes,
He took the brownness of a chestnut,
He took the clearness from still water,
He took the sparkle of a thousand stars.

From a tower,
He took the silence of the empty corridor,
He took the dampness of the walls,
He took the blackness of the ceiling,
That made his face.

From a tree,
He took the leaves slowly falling to the ground,
He took the branches swaying in the breeze,
He took the movement of an animal running up a tree,
That made his walk.

Hannah Donkin (10)
Richmond House School

The Park

When we go to the park
The first thing I go on is the twisted ladder
Which is a ladder that is completely wrong.
Then I run for the swings
To go up and down and up.
If I'm not careful
I'll land straight in the muck.
Then I'm off to the slide
And when I get to the bottom
And hit the ground with a bump
I stand up and say,
'That really hurt my rump!'

Robin Butler (7)
Richmond House School

The Monkey

Its tail as strong as the trees themselves,
Swinging from tree to tree,
Always doing its job
That's not the only thing about a monkey.

Its arms are as important as anything,
Getting into fruit with its sharp claws,
Using its arms to swing on any branch,
That's not the only thing about a monkey.

Its razor-sharp teeth,
That can bite any fruit
And can make the kill possible,
That's not the only thing about a monkey.

It squeals as loud as anything,
It pulls a face that can make you laugh,
And to look at he's hilarious,
That's the funniest thing about a monkey.

Joe Whitehurst (11)
Richmond House School

Bonfire Night

Bonfire crackling all night long
Rockets are banging all night long
The flames are orange, the flames are red
Sparks are crackling overhead
I don't mind but one just landed on my head!
So now . . . I am dead.

Jonathan Webster (7)
Richmond House School

Tortillas, Tortillas

Tortillas! Tortillas!
You are so divine,
You are so nice,
You are all mine.

Tortillas! Tortillas!
You are so big,
You are so very nice,
But not like a twig.

Tortillas! Tortillas!
I love the flour,
On my tongue,
It gives me power.

Tortillas! Tortillas!
You are so nice,
A bit like egg fried rice.

William Harrison (10)
Richmond House School

Train, Train

Train, train,
Go round and round,
Train, train,
Go up and down,
Train, train,
Say hello,
Train, train,
You're going too slow,
Train, train,
Say bye-bye,
Train, train,
It's beddy byes.

Keyanur Bennett (10)
Richmond House School

Ode To Chow Mein

Chow mein, chow mein,
You're delicious, divine,
I love you a lot,
And you are all mine!
You're sloshy and slishy,
You have lots of noodles,
And chicken galore,
I have you in oodles.

Chow mein, chow mein,
You're nicer than nice,
You're piled on my plate,
On top of the rice!
Chow mein, chow mein,
You're as good as can be,
You're juicy and slippy,
Just right for me!

Molly Smith (9)
Richmond House School

Pizza, Pizza

Pizza, pizza,
Your chillies are so bright,
I just can't stop thinking about you,
All night,
Pizza, pizza,
Your cheese is like gold,
You can't get away from me,
I love it when you fold.

Josef Baczkowski (9)
Richmond House School

Chocolate Cake!

Chocolate cake! Chocolate cake!
You are so nice,
When I eat you straight from the freezer,
You are as cold as ice.
Chocolate cake! Chocolate cake!
You are sticky and sweet,
You're gorgeous and dreamy,
And you're good to eat.

Chocolate cake! Chocolate cake!
I could eat you every day,
With lashings of cream,
But my mum says, 'No way.'
Chocolate cake! Chocolate cake!
I know you make me fat,
So I have decided,
To feed you to the cat.

Holly Stenton (10)
Richmond House School

Pizza, Oh Pizza

Pizza, oh pizza, oh Margarita pizza,
I'll go on my PC,
To buy you,
Oh I love you, so soft, chewy, cheesy and greasy.
Pizza, oh pizza, oh Margarita pizza,
I can taste the explosive chilli on the meat,
I love the cheating recipe,
I'm going to eat the taste of Latino heat.

Jayarjun Deu (9)
Richmond House School

The River

The river rushes by
Whoosh, whoosh
Over the stones
In its way.

Sun shines on the river
The fish glisten in the light
People walk in the mud
At the side of the river.

Flowers purple and yellow
Reeds green and brown
All grow
By the river.

Jessica Armstrong (8)
Richmond House School

Sausages

Roly-poly sausages in a pan
Fat and thin
Short and long
Pork ones, beef ones, herb ones and vegetarians
Sizzling in the pan, sizzling in the pan
Granny makes toad-in-the-hole, my favourite
Daddy loves sausages with brown sauce
And he likes them for his main course
Roly-poly sausages in a pan
Fat and thin
Short and long.

Aoife Jackson (7)
Richmond House School

I'm Not Howling!

Do you know there are ghosts in the night?
There are big green sharks walking
I'm not howling!
There are shadowy parts in the garden
Where the monsters pop out and say, *'Boo!'*
This makes us shriek
But I'm not howling!
Then I can see a shadowy shape
I yell, *'Aarrgghh!'*
But it's not a monster, it's Dad
He says, 'Go to sleep,' and goes away
Just as I stop howling
I see a hand creeping through the window
'Is it . . . is it? *Aarrgghh!'*
He raises his axe and . . . *chop!*
Then I wake up.

James Bastin (7)
Richmond House School

My Daddy

My daddy is funny because he sings in the shower
But doesn't have a very good voice
My daddy is silly because he has pillow fights
And he jumps off the bed
My daddy makes me laugh when he tickles me
My daddy is kind and loving and gives me lots of hugs
My daddy is the best daddy in the world.

Amelia Mary Crump (7)
Richmond House School

Roo And Belephant In The Zoo

Roo was a baby kangaroo
Whose mummy was called Ellie
Roo ran around the zoo
And slept in his mummy's belly.

The pouch was lovely and warm at night
Roo stayed there until it became light
Then he would stretch and run and play
Around the zoo all day.

Roo's special friend was Belephant
He was a baby elephant
He was much bigger but not faster than Roo
They both had much fun around the zoo.

Sam Kavanagh (7)
Richmond House School

One Laughing Leopard

One laughing leopard leaping on the land.
Two terrified turtles torturing in a band.

Three thirsty thrushes feasting on a dish.
Four fat frogs fishing for some fish.

Five freaky foxes frying in the sun.
Six sweet swallows sleeping and having fun.

Seven swans swimming softly in the sea.
Eight excited eels getting annoyed by a bee.

Nine naughty nits picking on some hair.
Ten terrifying tigers running after a bear.

Nayab Chaudhry (10)
Richmond House School

A Dog

Look at that dog,
Over there,
Slinking quietly,
Through the night.

Look at that dog,
Over there,
Barking at that old lady.

Look at that dog,
Over there,
Cleaning its fur,
With its paws.

Look at that dog,
Over there,
His brown eyes,
Glowing in the dark.

Look at that dog,
Over there,
His tongue panting,
Like he has just been on a run.

Fred Kamstra (11)
Richmond House School

Pizza

Pizzas, pizzas on a little plate.
Red little pizza on a little plate.
Pizzas, pizzas are so great.
Pizzas, pizzas are my mate.

Edward Sargeant (7)
Richmond House School

It Was Made

It was made
From sewer slime
It took the green glow
From radiation

Its eyes were made
From balls of fire
Its tongue was made
From human flesh

Its teeth were made from
Diamond stone
Its strength was taken
From a hundred trucks

And now it's ready to storm the town.

James Wilson (11)
Richmond House School

When I Went . . .

When I went to the airport,
I saw this strange old man,
I thought he looked quite old,
In fact he was covered in ham.

When I went to the hospital,
They gave me some laughing gas,
They said, 'You must be faking it,
But you're a funny lass!'

Chantelle Joslin (10)
Richmond House School

Lemon Cake! Lemon Cake!

Lemon cake! Lemon cake!
You're lovely and creamy,
You're great in my tum,
You make me go dreamy.
Lemon cake! Lemon cake!
You're delicious and sweet,
You're circular and mellow,
I have you as a treat.

Lemon cake! Lemon cake!
You're delicious and tangy,
You're dusted with sugar,
And I eat you when I'm watching Bambi.
Lemon cake! Lemon cake!
You're magic and sour,
You're round not square,
I even eat you in the shower.

Lemon cake! Lemon cake!
You're squidgy and fluffy,
When I watch TV,
You sometimes remind me of Buffy.
Lemon cake! Lemon cake!
I've had enough of you now,
I used to like you lots,
But now I think you're foul.

Sian Gatenby (10)
Richmond House School

Superman's Day Out

Football funky Superman
Got knocked over by a ram
Went to Chile
Got a bit silly
And that was the end of poor Superman.

Gosha Smith (7)
Richmond House School

One Woeful Warthog

One woeful warthog sitting under a tree.
Two tiny tarantulas catching a tiny flea.

Three treacherous tigers killing terribly.
Four fat turtles singing merrily.

Five frightened cubs hiding from the pack.
Six slithering snakes looking for a snack.

Seven slimy slugs leaving a trail.
Eight elegant emus hiding in a bale.

Nine nasty nits itching for a drink.
Ten tall turtles all covered in pink.

Eleven enormous elephants bathing in the lake.
Twelve twittering thrushes scratching like a rake.

Thirteen tricky turtles waiting for their prey.
Fourteen fragile frogs swimming away.

Fifteen fantastic flamingos flying through the air.
Sixteen special swallows hiding in their lair.

Anthony West (10)
Richmond House School

One, Two And Three

One orange orang-utan swings from tree to tree,
Two tiny tortoises swimming in the sea.

Three stupid snakes slithering on a log,
Four fat frogs chasing a big dog.

Five dangerous dogs catching a cat,
Six smelly mice which were caught in a sack.

Seven beautiful baboons eating a rat,
Eight cute kittens sitting on a mat.

Nine nits running everywhere,
Ten tiny termites eating a large pear.

Jennie Stubbs (10)
Richmond House School

How The Whale Began

The whale began when
He took the smoothness of silk
He took the sliminess of a snail
To make his skin

For his eyes
He took the sharpness of an eagle
He took the brightness of night flies

For his colour
He took the greyness of a seal
He took the blueness of the night sky

For his teeth
He took the sharpness of a tiger's teeth
And the whiteness of a polar bear

For his movement
He took the slowness of a turtle
He took the weight of one thousand seals.

Malkit Sihra (10)
Richmond House School

There Was An Old Man In Leeds

There was an old man in Leeds
Who really loved looking at bees.
When stung on the nose
While smelling a rose
He blew one away with a sneeze.

William Peckham (9)
Richmond House School

One Woozy Warthog

One woozy warthog bathing in the sun.
Two trembling turtles swimming in the Tum.

Three thirsty thistles waiting for the rain.
Four frenzied frogs lying in pain.

Five fluorescent flowers in a daydream.
Six silly snails all need to lean.

Seven stupid snakes lying all around.
Eight eager eagles chasing on the ground.

Nine know-it-all needles going through the cloth.
Ten tremendous tarantulas gnawing on a moth.

Molly Hayward (10)
Richmond House School

Counting Poem

One wobbly wombat winding down the road,
Two trailing tortoises carrying a load.

Three thoughtful turtles trundling through the sea,
Four fierce foxes lurking by a tree.

Five fancy fish flashing in the ocean,
Six slimy slugs sliding in slow motion.

Seven sly snakes slithering down the paths,
Eight enormous elephants learning the maths.

Nine nifty newts nipping through the lake,
Ten tired terrapins trying to stay awake.

Sebby May (10)
Richmond House School

Ode To Chocolate

Chocolate! Chocolate!
I love you a lot,
You make me feel good,
Even when I am not.
Chocolate! Chocolate!
Just look at that bill,
When I buy you,
It is always a thrill.

Chocolate! chocolate!
You are brilliantly good,
I can't keep my eyes off you,
Even when I should,
Chocolate! Chocolate!
You need to give me a break,
I know you really love me,
But it's all I can take.

Chocolate! Chocolate!
Brown, nutty and white,
They are all so tasty,
I love eating them all on Bonfire Night.
Chocolate! Chocolate!
I need you right now,
Oh, how I love you,
I will get you somehow.

Simran Bhullar (9)
Richmond House School

Water

Water, water in a lake
Running down to the sea
Home to lots of fish and ducks
My favourite place to be.

Hannah Gatenby (8)
Richmond House School

Animal Mania

One wobbly wombat dancing in the rain
Two trembling tigers crying out in pain

Three lazy lions lying in the sun
Four silly seals having lots of fun

Five furry foxes rolling in the mud
Six horrible hyenas sucking a deer's blood

Seven raging rabbits bouncing on a hill
Eight sick stick insects feeling ill

Nine huge horses race around the barn
Ten grumpy gorillas try to keep calm

Eleven miserable monkeys sulk in a tree
Twelve elegant eels gliding through the sea

Thirteen clumsy cows graze in the meadow
Fourteen spiteful sparrows hiding in the hedgerow

Fifteen cute cats sitting on the wall
Sixteen perky puppies race for the ball

Seventeen gentle giraffes standing tall and proud
Eighteen pretty parrots singing aloud

Nineteen eager eagles searching for their prey
Twenty mischievous mice burrowing in the hay.

Charlotte Barraclough (11)
Richmond House School

My Sister

My sister's kind, my sister's gentle
If you believe that you must be mental
My sister's bossy, my sister's mean
When it comes to bullying my sister's keen
She tells tales about me
I'll get her back, just wait and see
My sister thinks she is my mother
Goodness knows I don't need another!

James Richert (9)
Richmond House School

Monsters

Monsters can be big,
Monsters can be small,
Monsters can also be very tall.
Monsters can be fat,
Monsters can be thin,
And they can eat stuff from the bin.

Monsters can be naughty,
Monsters can be nice,
Monsters sometimes can be very bright.
Monsters can be dull,
Monsters can be fun,
Monsters can fight,
Monsters can be calm,
Monsters are cool,
Monsters are smart,
Some of them can see in the dark.

Monsters can fly,
Monsters can walk,
Some monsters even talk,
Monsters are honest,
Monsters lie,
But altogether they are very nice.

Hugo Calder (8)
Richmond House School

Oh Pizza! Oh Pizza!

Oh pizza! Oh pizza!
So crispy is your crust,
All your melted cheese,
I have to eat you, I must.
You're splodged with tomatoes,
All juicy, ripe and red,
Oh pizza! Oh pizza!
I gobble you up in bed.

Zac Campsall-Bhatti (10)
Richmond House School

Chocolate

I really like something
Beginning with C

It's not caramel or cream
It's not Coke or cheese
Nor cookies
If you please

I like it because
It's milky and sweet
Sometimes for me
It's a very big treat

It's munchy and crunchy
And very nice
It goes down my throat
In a trice

It's very creamy
And utterly dreamy
It's scrummy and yummy
And fills my tummy

I really like something
Beginning with C
Yes, the thing for me
Is *chocolate!*

Joe Kamstra (9)
Richmond House School

Crisps

Crisps are the best,
Oh yes they are!
They're better than the rest,
By far, far, far!

They're crispy and tasty,
And ever so salty,
To me they're a treat,
They never are faulty.

Their taste is great,
It fills me with mirth,
The taste is so wondrous
It's like Heaven on Earth!

There's hundreds of flavours like
Cheese and onion
Ready salted
And prawn cocktail.
Great though they are,
My favourite by far,
The only star is
Salt
And
Vinegar!

Every Wednesday,
I go to the shop,
And open my crisps,
Pop!

Davy Ker (9)
Richmond House School

My Horse

I have always wished for a horse,
My parents said, 'One day, darling, of course.'

One Saturday my wish came true,
That day I wasn't blue.

I called my horse Blaze,
He is so beautiful I am in a daze.

He flies over the jump,
Without even a bump.

He is amazing at trot,
I love him a lot.

Lottie McMahon (9)
Richmond House School

Trees

Trees, they give us O^2
Trees, we cut them right through
We chop down the old
But don't always replace them with new

Trees, they grow up like me and you
Trees have a life just as we do
We will die out before the trees
They will go on, just you see.

Joshua Frazer (9)
Richmond House School

What Do Parents Do All Day?

What do parents do all day?
Do they scream and shout?
I know they tell off their children
That's without a doubt.

What do parents do all day?
Do they dream that they're a child
Running through the fields
Acting as if they were wild?

What do parents do all day?
Do they explore
Or maybe they paint?
But I'm sure there's a lot more.

What do parents do all day?
Do they sit in a chair and snore
Or maybe they dream?
But I'm sure they're a bore.

What do parents do all day?
Do they spend the day bleaching the loo
Or maybe they nag me till I turn blue?
What do parents do?

Matthew Chan (10)
Richmond House School

Wolf

The wolf began approaching
Its beady eyes turned and tossed side to side
Its shimmering tail wagged up and down
It silently approached its prey
And then it pulled its sharp claws up above its prey and
Bang!
Its sharp, jagged teeth burst into its prey
The animal panicking
Eventually the animal was dead.

Jac Moore (11)
Richmond House School

Monsters

I know a monster
Who's really strong
I know a monster
Who can play ping-pong

I know a monster
With a screechy laugh
I know a monster
Who lives in a bath

I know a monster
Who can fly in the sky
I know a monster
Who can make cranberry pie

I know a monster
With a big smile
I know a monster
Who can run a mile

I know a monster
He lives in my bed
I know a monster
And he's my big ted.

Marcus Gay (9)
Richmond House School

The Day My Cat Died

My cat ran down the stairs
And landed on the mat

She shot out of the door
Because she couldn't take it anymore

She didn't look where she was going
And without her knowing

She dashed out in front of a car
And got knocked all the way to a bar.

Luke Richert (9)
Richmond House School

Chips, Oh Chips

Chips, oh chips
Salty and crunchy
You make me fat at my hips
You're a million times better than Monster Munchy.

Chips, oh chips
You make me drool all day long
The name just makes me lick my lips
I just couldn't be wrong.

Chips, oh chips
You break in my mouth
You look like yellow whips
You're made in the south.

Wonderful chips
Please never change
Stay here forever
And I'll always have a mouth-watering crave!

Charlotte Martin (10)
Richmond House School

Spiders

Spiders are creepy
And very sneaky.
They come in different sizes
Huge, massive and *humungous.*

Spiders are like a nightmare
You turn around and they're there.
They hide in the shower
And maybe the bath.

Spiders can give you a nasty nip
And here's a handy tip.
Put a bowl of conkers in your room at night
To stop them giving you a nasty fright.

Alexandra Lawrence (9)
Richmond House School

Caribbean Casserole

Caribbean casserole
You're as yummy as can be
You make my mouth water
You're peppery and sweet.

You're yummy and scrummy
And spicy as can be!
I could eat plates and plates of you
I like you because you're creamy.

You're magic and so sloshy
I'd eat you till I die.
I love your bright orange sauce
It really is divine!

Caribbean casserole
I love you for my tea
I really couldn't share you
You're just for me, me, me!

Molly Jane Harper (10)
Richmond House School

School Lunch!

School dinners are munchy, crunchy and great,
The tasty food is smothered all over my plate.
There is chips, chicken, chocolate and more,
But sometimes school dinners can be a bore.
The pasta is yummy, it's slurpy and hot,
The dinner ladies are kind because they give us a lot.
They are nutritious and healthy I do believe,
I will keep having school dinners until I leave.
School dinners are wonderful!

Gemma Richert (9)
Richmond House School

Being A Twin

I am a twin
Some say I am the quiet one
My sister
She never stops talking . . .
Always making a din.
My sister laughs like a drain
She shouts like a fishwife
She giggles like a hyena
She can be a real pain.
I love my sister though
Because she is clever
She is jolly
She is full of energy
And she is
My twin!

Hayden Ronan Rawlins (10)
Richmond House School

My Cute Baby Sister

My cute baby sister
I love to kiss her
She's sweet and jolly
She claps her hands in joy
She crawls on the floor
She loves her food
She loves her teddy
My cute baby sister
I love to kiss her.

Maheen Nadir (10)
Richmond House School

My Little Brother Haaris

My little brother Haaris
Does a lot to embarrass
Me.
He takes my toys
Typical of boys.
He takes my money
And thinks it's funny.
He's messy with his food
And gets in a mood.
But would I change him . . . ?
Yes!

Anum Ahmed (9)
Richmond House School

Handbags

I have a passion
For fashion
I love my handbags
They have hefty price tags

I have pink ones
Purple ones, orange and red
I love them so much
I take them to bed.

Francesca Birley (9)
Richmond House School

P

P is for purple,
P is for peach,
P is for perfect,
Just like me!

P is for pretty,
P is for perfume,
P is for playful,
Just like me!

P is for posh,
P is for poser,
P is for proud,
Just like me!

P is for pink,
P is for passion,
P is for popular.

Enough about me!
What about you?

Felicity Rudd (10)
Richmond House School

Cricket Poem

Cricket is fun
It's number one
Cricket is great
Like your mate.

The umpire's the boss,
He sometimes gets cross
He wears a white coat
And appears remote.

Cricket is my life
Without it really I would be full of strife.

Amar Patel (9)
Richmond House School

Chocolate! Chocolate!

Chocolate! Chocolate!
You're so divine
Oh wonderful chocolate
Why can't you be mine?
You have lots of sugar
You're sweet and crunchy
Chocolate! Chocolate!
Stay here with me.

Chocolate! Chocolate!
Cut into squares
Or put in a Mars bar
With caramel layers
When you're on my plate
I can't resist you
Chocolate! Chocolate!
Love you I do.

Chocolate! Chocolate!
Lovely and clean
You're so special
You're fit for the Queen
You make me smile
You can ice my cake
Chocolate! Chocolate!
How much can I take?

Katherine J Ward (9)
Richmond House School

Down Below The Staircase

Down below the staircase
There is a smelly shoe
It's been there for many years
It makes us all feel ill.

Alicia Jeavons (10)
Richmond House School

Ode To Chocolate Chip Cookies

Chocolate chip cookies
I couldn't live without,
They're soft and they're chewy,
And yummy no doubt.

Chocolate chip cookies,
They're divine and sweet,
They're full of tastiness,
Lots I could eat.

Chocolate chip cookies,
They're big and round,
They're a beautiful gold,
And chocolate is found.

Chocolate chip cookies,
I take a big bite,
And in my mind,
It's a beautiful sight.

Chloe Ramsden (10)
Richmond House School

Sport

I used to play mini tennis,
And now I play full court tennis.
You play cricket,
With a wicket.
You also play with a bat,
And you wear a hat.
You play baseball with a small ball,
You practise football,
Against a wall.

Rufus Mitchell (8)
Richmond House School

Galaxy! Galaxy!

Galaxy! Galaxy!
You're my favourite chocolate bar
I love you, Galaxy
You're my No 1 star
You're smooth, you're silky
You melt in my mouth
I don't know where you come from
I think you're from the south!

Galaxy! Galaxy!
You're wrapped in gold foil
With luxurious cream lettering
You're just pure royal
When I unwrap you
You look so inviting
I can't wait to eat you
It's just so exciting!

Galaxy! Galaxy!
You're creamy and divine
You're explosive and magic
I'm so lucky you're mine
You're going to be eaten now
It's my big treat
I wish there was more
It's so scrummy to eat!

Imogen Kaberry (10)
Richmond House School

Sweets

Sugary sweets cause rotting teeth to a little fellow
But if they're black they can be much worse than that.

Hugh Kelly (7)
Richmond House School

Oh Toffee, Oh Toffee

Oh toffee, oh toffee,
So chewy and divine,
Oh toffee, oh toffee,
I could eat you *any* time.
You're hard on the outside,
But I know you so well,
You're soft on the inside,
And there's lots more to tell!

Oh toffee, oh toffee,
Tons and gallons of the stuff,
So incredible I ignore my mum,
When she says, 'You've had enough!'
You explode in my mouth,
Then melt to a stop,
But the taste is still there,
I could eat you till I *pop!*

Oh toffee, oh toffee,
So creamy and fine,
Oh toffee, oh toffee,
Why can't you be mine?
You're golden and smooth,
Creamy and magic,
If I lost you,
It would just be tragic!

Isabel Kempner (10)
Richmond House School

The Tiger

T he tiger sits and waits for his prey
I n the jungle in the heat of May
G rowling softly he spies a zebra
E xtremely strong, he runs on and on
R oaring when his prey has gone.

Julien Abensour (8)
Richmond House School

Ice Cream! Ice Cream!

Ice cream! Ice cream!
You taste so divine
You're creamy and mellow
Why can't you be mine?
Sprinkled with chocolate
Or strawberry sauce
You taste sweet and lovely
I'll get you by force!

Ice cream! Ice cream!
Up to the sky
Big spoonfuls of ice cream
I can't say goodbye!
Lick it and slurp it
It drips on your chin
Shout for more, shout for more
Oh! What a din!

Ice cream! Ice cream!
On a hot day
You get really runny
And I say, *'Hooray!'*
I eat you all up
You taste so divine
Ice cream! Ice cream!
Why can't you be mine?

Harriet Liddington (9)
Richmond House School

Footie Champion

F ootie is a fantastic game
O h, how I love it
O li is my brother's name
T o be a great sport for me
  To be a fantastic footballer is my dream
I hope one day I am one
E ven though I'm a girlie.

Rachel Dixon (7)
Richmond House School

Chocolate

Oh chocolate, oh chocolate
You make me melt,
Oh chocolate, oh chocolate
You break my belt.
You're lovely and creamy,
You make me go dreamy
You go crunch,
I don't want my lunch.
Oh chocolate, oh chocolate
You make me feel sick,
Oh chocolate, oh chocolate
I still give you a lick.
You make me go big,
So I can't play tig.
Maybe I'll die
Or just switch to pie.
Oh chocolate, oh chocolate, oh chocolate.

Elizabeth Crocker (9)
Richmond House School

Samosas, Samosas

Samosas, samosas,
You're so divine,
You're a taste desire
And you are all mine.

Samosas, samosas,
The microwave goes *ping*.
You're so mouth-watering
And the price, *kerching!*

Samosas, samosas,
You're bumpy but soft,
You're triangular and yellow
And I can't get enough.

Ben Chand (10)
Richmond House School

My Friend Chloe!

My friend Chloe wears two pigtails
And as a friend she never fails
She dances, she prances
She's worth the world
A friendship valued more than pearls

My friend Chloe has big blue eyes
And my friend Chloe hardly ever lies
Imagine if she was my sister
But if she left, boy, would I miss her

My friend Chloe is the best around
She's someone to depend on I have found
It's nice to have a pal like her
This gal's rated more than myrrh.

Renuka Rawlins (10)
Richmond House School

Snow

A tongue - taster
A nose - tickler
A formation - builder
A wall - maker
An enemy - weapon
A sky - filler
A colour - taker
A shape - sailer
A rain - replacer
An ice - former
A neck - chiller
An ice - speck
A plant - coverer.

James Griffiths (10)
Richmond House School

Space

When I grow up
I want to fly even
Further than the sky.
I want to find
My own place even
Further than space.
I want to
Explore
Jupiter
Saturn
And
Lots, lots more.
I will find
My own galaxy
Milky Way
And Mars.
Talking about
Chocolate I
Feel a bit hungry.
Maybe I'll be a fat
Man when I'm a tiny
Bit older.

James Gilman (9)
Richmond House School

My Kangaroo

My kangaroo is called Jake.
He jumps very high.
He lives in a very big house.
He's got a fantastic shop.
He sometimes is happy.
He's sometimes good and sometimes bad
And now he's brilliant.

Anisah Khan (7)
Richmond House School

Wild Animals

Elephant
I once saw an elephant walking in the wild
With his big mouth, it gave me a smile.
Then he charged towards me with his big tusks
But got me, only just.

Giraffe
I once saw a giraffe walking in the wild,
It was tall and spotty
And its coat was all blotty.

Crocodile
I once saw a crocodile swimming in the wild.
It was green, it was scaly,
It was a reptile.

Lewis Vincent (9)
Richmond House School

Dogs

Dogs are big, dogs are small.
Dogs are tiny, dogs are tall.
Dogs are weak, dogs are strong
And you see them running along.

Dogs are boring, dogs are funny.
Dogs can be very cunning.
Dogs are short, dogs are long
And you see them running along.

Dogs are smelly, dogs are clean.
Dogs are keen where others have been.
Dogs are old, dogs are young.
Dogs can be very fun!

George Barker (9)
Richmond House School

Monsters

Monsters are big, monsters are tall
And also can be very small.
Monsters are long, monsters are thin
But none of them can really sing.
Monsters are honest, monsters tell lies
And all of them eat some pies.
Monsters are dark, monsters are bright
And when you look at them it is light.
Monsters are rough, monsters are smooth
And some of them have a booth.
Monsters are nasty, monsters are nice
And also eat their pet mice.
Monsters sleep in a box, monsters sleep in a bed
And all the ones that sleep in a bed are called Fred.
Monsters are hairy, monsters are bold
And all the ones that are bold can all fold.
Monsters are thick, monsters are smart
And some of them fly like a dart.
Monsters are early, monsters are late
And some of them always faint.
Monsters are brave, monsters are afraid
And some of them misbehave.

George Hall (9)
Richmond House School

Uncle Harry Back From War

Uncle Harry back from war.
Uncle Harry's at the door.
Uncle Harry, will you play with me
Or can we play Monopoly?
Uncle Harry is very nice
After tea we played a game of *dice!*

Oliver Wilson (9)
Richmond House School

My Pets

Bay Bow is my cute little poodle
He's very quiet though
He can be very loud
And when he is loud
I give him a pink bow

My cat Pat spends most of her time
Lying on the doormat
My old, fat cat

I have a rabbit called Flipper
One day he went outside in my slippers
Then he went to see
My other rabbit Melody
And they came back from Halifax
To get a hat.

Holly Wilson (9)
Richmond House School

It's There

I've got a monster in my house
Running everywhere
I always try and get a pear but he is always there.

I always try and get to bed
But he is always there
So I end up screaming and running everywhere.

I try and watch the telly
But he is always there
So I switch it off and start running everywhere.

I think it is a ghost
'Cause it always steals the post.

Toby Ambrose Ellison-Scott (8)
Richmond House School

My First Time On A Snowboard

Wrapped up warm
Sitting on the snow
Excited to get up on the board and *go!*

All I see is multicoloured skiers
Feeling worried as they rush past me
All I can think about is staying off my knees!

Snowboarding is wave boarding but not on sea, on snow
As I surfed down the mountain, twisting and turning
I really felt I was learning!

A bump in the snow made me lose my balance
I was tumbling and falling and slipping and sliding
Snow was everywhere, even in my hair!
I think I need a few more lessons but I haven't lost hope!

Zack Bambage (9)
Richmond House School

Space

Space is big, planets are small like a boy on the wall.
It is good in space, you can play all sorts of games.
Saturn is big but Earth is small.
Pluto is cold but Mercury is hot.
Space has stars, the moon, the lot.
Earth is cool, smart and shines in the dark
But the other planets are slightly stark.
Earth is living but the other planets are dead
Like a bird in the shed.

Charles Moran (8)
Richmond House School

A Gruesome Ghost

When you walk down the path
You'll see a gruesome ghost quite fast
Slimy green and bright red head
Shimmering scales, flowery tails
That's the ghost that lives on the path.

When you walk down the path
You'll see a gruesome ghost quite fast
Roaring, tumbling, ghostly sounds
You'll be quite amazed
And rolling on its thighs.

When you walk down the path
You'll see a gruesome ghost quite fast
You'll be amazed at its thrilling chase
On the way to school
Boo! Unfortunately it's after you!

Jessica Lloyd (8)
Richmond House School

Names

Clarey Clogs lives on Hairy Lane.
She's got a hairy house just like a mouse
And it's a horrible house indeed.

Janey Jogs lives on Painy Lane.
Her house feels pain
And it's crying every day indeed.

Shaney Shack lives on Shacky Lane.
It shakes every day non-stop
So it's shaky every day.

Angelita Michael (8)
Richmond House School

Autumn Is Here!

As I walk I see red, yellow and brown
And sometimes I see leaves falling down.
The autumn wind blows and I start putting on warm clothes.
The nights are getting darker, the mist is getting thicker
And I know autumn is here!

Hallowe'en with scary noises is part of autumn as well
And bonfires make a smell
With fireworks as big as boulders
And fireworks as small as pencil holders.
Different colours, red, yellow and brown
Somebody nearly fainted and they fell down.
The sounds are louder than an elephant
Stamping his feet
And the sounds of a mouse when he squeaks.
They go *boom, crackle* and *pop!*
The Catherine wheels never stop!

Autumn reminds me of the conker tournaments with friends
And the many battles I try to win.
I love the game of harvest festival, a time for giving
To charities all over the world - I collect food with a grin!

Alex Shaw (8)
Richmond House School

There Was A Fat Lady From Leeds

There was a fat lady from Leeds
Who had a beautiful string of beads
One day she was shopping
The beads started hopping
All over the city of Leeds.

Natalie Brykalski (9)
Richmond House School

Fox Was Created

It was created
With its golden orange fur from the sun,
Its smoothness from metal coins
And that's its coat.

For its teeth
They took knives and over years
They've worn away
And made teeth.

For its eyes
It took lava from a volcano,
Hot and red and ready to pounce
And that's its eyes.

For its slyness
It took the quietness from a night sky
And the cunningness from a hyena,
That made its slyness.

Coat,
Teeth,
Eyes,
Slyness.

A fox!

Mike Wren-Kirkham   (10)
Richmond House School

Too Cool To Be In School!

I'm too cool to be in school,
I gel my hair like a spike,
On a bike.
My teachers are cool,
My headmaster is a fool,
I'm too cool to be in school!

Gurnam Singh Badesha   (8)
Richmond House School

The Dragon Lives

The wings were made from the roughness of the bark.
The brown from the leaves.
The beat from the water.

For the teeth he took the sharpness from the knife.
He took a bit of the moon for the shiny glint.
The bite from the earthquake.

His breath from the sun.
The smell from the rotting food.
The destruction from an atomic bomb.

His eyes from raging flames.
The brightness from the moon.
The brownness from the leaves.

The tail's brown from a tree.
The sharpness from the arrow.
The length from a mountain.

Dominic Hartley (11)
Richmond House School

The Haunted House

The haunted house is a scary place
With ghosts and monsters too.
The dingy gates are always dim
And always going, *'Boo!'*
When you go in you'll get a fright
And never come out again.
The ghost will catch you and you'll end up in his den.

Nicholas Winn (8)
Richmond House School

Water Mania

An apple caused a ripple
As it fell into a puddle
It splashed a lady passing by
I said, 'What a muddle!'

She said, 'My clothes are soaking wet,'
And then began to wriggle
She looked so funny in her rage
That I began to giggle.

I said, 'Beware of wobbly fruits
That soon begin to topple.
Next time it could be you that's hit
And not the little puddle!'

James Micklethwaite (7)
Richmond House School

Kicker The Kangaroo

Kicker is a kangaroo,
His legs as big as mine.
He lives in my wardrobe,
And always bounces about.
He is very big,
But my parents cannot see him.
He is very noisy,
But my parents cannot hear him.
He is very smelly,
But my parents cannot smell him,
Because he is *imaginary!*

Rory Denison (8)
Richmond House School

Dinosaurs

Thumping feet,
In the heat.
Fearsome roar,
At the door.
Nostrils flaring,
Never caring.
Burning eyes,
Like stormy skies.
Stinky breath,
The smell of death.
Extinct at last,
Because of a blast!

Holly Lenahan (7)
Richmond House School

Funky Monkey

I saw a funky monkey.
He's very, very jumpy.
He jumps around with a crown.
Clunky! Clunky! Clunky!
He's very, very jumpy
And very, very funky.
He jumps around with a frown.
Clunky! Clunky! Clunk!

Matthew Harris (9)
Richmond House School

The Crocodile

There is a giant crocodile
Who lives in the River Nile
He slides off the muddy riverbanks
He swims slowly and silently up the river
Shush . . . he sees something moving in the water
He smells something tasty
Snap! as he darts across the water
And gobbles it down in one gulp.

William Masterton (8)
Richmond House School

Sunshine

This is a thing that can't go away,
To see it you don't have to pay,
We sometimes see it in the day,
When it comes out to play,
But at night you think it's gone,
You won't be thinking it for long,
Before I tell you what it is,
All I want to say is this,
It's the one we can't live without,
I can say this without a doubt,
I think you know what I'm talking about . . .

Sunshine!

Sam Crossley (10)
Roberttown J&I School

Who Am I?

Who am I?
Am I an elegant dancer
Waiting to perform?
Who am I?
Am I the best sports champion
Waiting to be born?

Who am I?
Am I the caring animal lover
Treating every one as my own?
Who am I?
Am I the one who is always eager to help
But who hates to be alone?

Who am I?
Am I the girl filled with fun and laughter
And always ready with a loving smile?
Who am I?
I am *that* girl who you can always trust
More than once in a while.

Kellie-Jo Jeffery (10)
Roberttown J&I School

Guitar

My best possession
Has no expression
It really is a star.

It makes loads of noise
Mostly used by boys
It is my guitar.

Sam Bull (11)
Roberttown J&I School

The Bobbins

In the land of the Bobbins
The bahambo bush grows
They eat tea at breakfast and breakfast at tea
They eat supper at lunch and lunch at supper!
Their shadow does not follow them
It goes the other way instead!

In the land of the Bobbins
No trees dare grow
No, no trees dare grow
The Bobbins do not sleep
Yes, the Bobbins do not sleep, sleep, sleep.
The Bobbins do not sleep.

Kirsty Crowther (10)
Roberttown J&I School

The Future

In the future there'll be hover cars,
And you'll be able to reach the stars.

In the future people will live in lakes,
And everyone will eat cakes.

In the future we won't go to school,
We'll stay in the pool.

In the future,
In the future.

Laylaa Whittaker (10)
Roberttown J&I School

My Cats

Rascal,
A food craver,
Eating, eating, eating,
Eating all the food in her sight.

My cats

Custard,
A cuddly cat,
Walking, jumping, climbing,
Sleeping on my bed through the day.

My cats

Tui,
So very old,
Sleeping, climbing, eating,
Always grumpy with the kittens.

My cats.

Joshua Glassett (10)
Roberttown J&I School

Sunset

Orange, very warm
Sinking, falling, drifting
Drifting slowly into the hills.

Sun.

Olivia Ledgard (11)
Roberttown J&I School

I Would Like To Hear . . .

I would like to hear
The grass sway from
Side to side.
I would like to hear
A photo frame crack.
I would like to hear
A window smash.
I would like to hear
A cat's bones smack.
I would like to hear
The tapping of a keyboard.
I would like to hear
The sound of a recorder or ocarina.
I would like to hear
The donkey's bells.
I would like to hear
The vacuum cleaner.

Brittany Stead (8)
Roberttown J&I School

Rainbow

I stand in one place looking up above
At the beautiful colours of the rainbow.
Violet, pink and orange
The magnificent arch above me.
I wonder where it will go?
What is at the other side?

Maybe a pot of gold.
The thing is . . . will I ever know?

Amy Peacock (10)
Roberttown J&I School

Our Dream Horse

O ur horse is the best
U pon a saddle I sit
R acing through the wind

D irty in the stable
R ough in the field
E legant when riding
A ce when jumping
M y dream horse

H onest and trusting
O ur horse is as green as grass
R iding in the barn
S ummertime is coming
E verlasting days.

I wake up
Where is my dream horse?

Kirsty Gee & Rachel Secker (10)
Roberttown J&I School

One Morning

One misty, moisty morning
On Crockendale Farm
There was a little chicken
Who lived inside a barn!

His mother called him Cheeky
His father called him Lucky
His brothers and sisters did not know
So they just called him Ducky!

Ellen Bellfield (10)
Roberttown J&I School

A Journey Through My Senses

I would like to smell the water
As it slowly weaves in and out
And dodges the rocks in its path.
I would like to hear the clouds
As they slowly drift in and out of the sky
And get pushed about in the wind.
I would like to touch the sky
As it changes different colours
Day and night
And brings it into my hands.
I would like to hear the stones
As they get washed away
In the rough water.

Sam Gaunt (7)
Roberttown J&I School

Pluto

Pluto is an ice palace
Sitting there day and night
The sun is a pinprick in the distance.

Deserted and alone orbiting the sun
Man has never touched Pluto's surface
And that's just how I want it to be.

I would love to live on Pluto
Just by myself
No town, no city.

Just me!

Georgina Barry (10)
Roberttown J&I School

Hide-And-Seek

There's the dog and the frog,
There's the mouse in his house,
There's the fox in a box,
There's the ape in a cape,
There's the hen in her pen.

There's the goose and the moose,
There's the snake in the cake,
There's the cat wearing her hat,
There's the skunk who got a bit drunk,
Then the brown bear got a big scare.

There's the pheasant being so pleasant,
There's the robin with a bobbin,
There's the sheep starting to creep,
There's the hare taking care,
There's the polar bear in his underwear.

There's the monkey getting funky,
There's the pig doing a jig,
There's the aardvark in the car park,
There's the duck in the muck,
And the kangaroo making a hullabaloo.

Then I saw the boar.

Lydia Glassett (8)
Roberttown J&I School

Untitled

River trickling drops of passion
Like lightning but really ice crystals
The sun comes out
The passion melts away but the love still stays.

Hamza Nawaz (9)
Roberttown J&I School

Dreams

A book is a place
    Where you can go
    Whenever you wish.
    Just open it up
    And step in.

For if you can read
    You can fight the Germans,
    Run through muddy trenches,
    Explore misty forests
    With your M16,
    Jump behind cover,
    Speak with Marshall,
    Hear bullets hit people and walls . . .

Have a break with your team
    Going through bottles of whiskey,
    Control a tank and . . .

When you come back
    Your clothes are clean,
    You lay there with scary
    Thoughts . . .

It's because you
    Know when you can go,
    Whenever you want,
    Anywhere you want.
    Just slide it open
    And step in again.

Connor Balach (10)
Roberttown J&I School

Frog

F linging about in the night
R otten frogs like to fight
O ver the moon they jump
G oing mad with lumpy humps.

Callum McDermott (8)
Roberttown J&I School

My Dad's Got A Motorbike!

My dad's got a motorbike!
It's shiny and it's red.
My mother doesn't like it much.
She thinks he's off his head!

He wears a helmet bright and red.
A jacket which is black.
A matching pair of leather trousers
That make him look quite fat!

His motorbike is loud and fast
As he rides it through our town.
People watch him speeding past
And give a glare and scowl!

'He is cool,' said all the school.
Dad went to top skills and won first prize
Then his motorbike shrank in size
And that's the end of that!

Emily Tench (8)
Roberttown J&I School

A Journey Through My Senses

I would love to touch the clouds
As they swerve around in the sky.
The giant clouds that move very, very slowly.
I would love to touch the sun
As it blazes with fire.
The beautiful red sun when it is moving in the sky.

James Ives (7)
Roberttown J&I School

My Blister

I have a blister
It looks like my sister
I wondered how I got it
I thought and thought
And then said, 'Maybe I should pop it'
I ran downstairs and cried
'Mum I've grown another nose!'
She grabbed and tugged with all her might
I let out a shriek, 'Mum you're holding too tight!'
My toes were clasped
Then the fierce woman gasped
'Is it sore?'
I said, in my head, *well by now it is raw.*
So in future don't tell your mum
You've got a spot of any shape or size
And don't tell your mum
Where it lives
Even if it's on your
Bum!

Bethany Stead (10)
Roberttown J&I School

A Journey Through My Senses

I wish I could touch the moon
I really, really want to touch it soon!
The moon is swirling, swirling around and around
Shining so bright
And everybody gets a fright!

James Thomas (8)
Roberttown J&I School

Waiting

Waiting for Christmas
Waiting for a tree
Waiting for the snow to fall,
So Santa can call.
Why do I have to wait?

Waiting for Rudolph,
Following his red nose
Waiting for a robin,
To come along a-bobbin.
Why do I have to wait?

I lay awake in my bed
Cuddling up to my big ted.
He is coming, on his way
To bring our presents on his sleigh.
Why do I have to wait, wait, wait?

Ellena Roberts (7)
Roberttown J&I School

The Ice Cream Monster

The ice cream monster is coming soon
To take all the ice cream vans.

It doesn't want crisps or sweets
Not even the massive Cola cans.

But it would be a pleasure to see this monster
Take all the ice cream.

Let's just hope that the ice cream monster
Hasn't got a wife called the Ice Cream Bonster!

Helen Edmond (9)
Roberttown J&I School

My Puppy

I've got a little puppy
His name is Alfie Shaw
It's really a little exciting
I've never had one before.

He runs around the garden
Playing with all of his toys
At times he seems a little silly
Just like all the boys.

He races up the stairs
Causing mayhem most of the day
He really doesn't seem to care
Cos he looks like a cuddly teddy bear.

Amber Shaw (8)
Roberttown J&I School

Roberttown School

R espectful
O pen
B est friends
E xceptional
R esponsible
T eam
T rustworthy
O bliging
W inners
N eighbourly

Roberttown School, my school.

Sara Jayne Pollard (11)
Roberttown J&I School

Ten Happy Schoolgirls

Ten happy schoolgirls all looking fine;
One had a zit
And then there were nine.

Nine happy schoolgirls all had mates;
One died
And then there were eight.

Eight happy schoolgirls all went up to Heaven;
One fell through a cloud
And then there were seven.

Seven happy schoolgirls chopping up sticks;
One chopped herself up
And then there were six.

Six happy schoolgirls playing round a hive;
One got stung
And then there were five.

Five happy schoolgirls went to saw;
One got eaten
And then there were four.

Four happy schoolgirls went to sea;
One got eaten by a shark
And then there were three.

Three happy schoolgirls put on a shoe;
One got their toe cut off
And then there were two.

Two happy schoolgirls didn't have any fun;
One got kidnapped
And then there was one.

One sad schoolgirl shrivelled in the sun;
Tried to run away
And then there were none.

Chelsea Mitchell (10)
Roberttown J&I School

A Journey Through My Senses

I would like to hear a whale,
The way it sounds under a rock,
How it squeaks in the water.
I would like to hear a lamp,
The sound of twinkling bulbs,
How they make it bright.

I would like to touch the clouds,
The bunchy cotton wool,
How it gets so spongy.
I would like to touch a star,
The sharp corners,
How it moves across the sky.

I would like to smell the air,
To smell what is in it,
How they get organised.
I would like to smell the moon,
How 'banana-ish' it could be,
The taste of all the edges too.

I would like to hear a picture
To find out who is who,
How to know who is my friend.
I would like to hear a clock,
To hear it go tick-tock, tick-tock,
And I would do it back.

Rachel Glaves (7)
Roberttown J&I School

A Journey Through My Senses

I'd like to touch a rainbow as the colour glows
I'd like to touch a rainbow as I touch my clothes
I'd like to touch a rainbow far away from London
I'd like to touch a rainbow
That's right
Yes!

Joseph Allatt (8)
Roberttown J&I School

Elements

Drip, drip, drip.
Water from the tap.
We drink the water.
We need the water
Drip, drip, drip.

Burn, burn, burn
Gives out heat for us.
We need the heat
We use the heat.
Burn, burn, burn.

Flash, flash, flash.
Lightning through the air
It hits the wire.
It snaps the wire.
Flash, flash, flash.

Swish, swish, swish.
Birds soaring in the sky.
We need the wind
We use the wind
Swish, swish, swish.

Charlotte Glaves (9)
Roberttown J&I School

Untitled

I would like to see a skiing dog
That wriggles and giggles.
I would like to smell a football
That moves about.

Callum Pickles (8)
Roberttown J&I School

Waiting For My Holiday

I'm waiting for my holiday,
I'm going to stay in a house.
I'm waiting for my holiday,
I hope there isn't a mouse.

I'm waiting for my holiday,
I'm going to play in the sand.
I'm waiting for my holiday,
I'll get it all over my hand.

I'm waiting for my holiday,
I'm going with my mum and my sister.
I'm waiting for my holiday,
We're going to go on the Twister.

I'm waiting for my holiday,
I'm going to go on a donkey.
I'm waiting for my holiday,
I hope it isn't wonky!

I'm waiting for my holiday,
I'm going to have lots of fun.
I'm waiting for my holiday,
But it feels like it will never come.

Jack Smith (7)
Roberttown J&I School

Midnight Magic

M idnight magic is in the air . . .
A mazing things begin to happen
G arden gnomes dance round the toadstools,
 I cicles glitter with fairy dust,
C ottages turn into enchanted castles.
A ll the garden is coming to life
L ittle fairies chasing in the moonlight.

Jennifer Hurst (8)
Roberttown J&I School

Winter Days

While I'd slept through the night
All the world had turned to white
A blanket of snow lay on the ground
No grass, no flowers to be found.
Snow on the road, garden hedge
There's even some on my window ledge.
I put on my wellies, coat and hat.
I build a snowman round and fat.
We throw snowballs at each other.
I try to throw mine at my brother.
I like the sun, the winter blow.
But best of all I like snow!

Ellie Walker (8)
Roberttown J&I School

Christmas

C hristmas is a time of year I enjoy
H olly leaves, angels and a brand new toy
R eindeer are fed as you go to bed
 I n preparation for their long trip ahead
S anta Claus is coming to town
T o find the chimneys he must climb down
M erry Christmas!
A t last!
S anta Claus is coming to town!

Robin Eloise Barraclough (7)
Roberttown J&I School

Friendship

Friendship is a star that runs just like a car.
It sometimes breaks down, but it always gets around town.
Friendship has a metallic coat of paint that will never fade.

Matthew Brook (11)
Roberttown J&I School

I Would Like . . .

I would like to smell a butterfly
Who flies in your ear with its wings out wide

So . . .

I would be so really still if I smelt a butterfly.

I would like to touch the moon but I know I can't.

So . . .

It would be really cool if I could touch the moon.

Alicia Kemp (7)
Roberttown J&I School

Swimming

S plashing around the noisy pool,
W ater's great to keep you cool,
I t's important to learn to swim,
M ight just save your life if you fall in!
M any types of different strokes,
I like backcrawl the most,
N oisy children all around,
G oing under to soften the sound.

Swimming!

Daniel Mott (10)
Roberttown J&I School

Fur Ball Friend

A cute face
A fast pace

Chew the table
Eat the label

Fetch the ball
Growing tall

Long walks
Yappy talks

A playful friend
In the end

Makes me
Bess the dog.

Daniel Collins (7)
Roberttown J&I School

Dragon

Deep in the depths of a cave
A dragon could be having a shave
It'll turn you into ash
Unless you're out of there in a flash
If you go there you're to blame
It will turn you into a flame.

James Ross & Alastair McDonald (10)
Roberttown J&I School

A Cinquain

Sheepy
Big balls of fluff
Simply walking around
They hate dogs, yet they lounge around.
Baa! Baa!

Robert Ives & David Hall (11)
Roberttown J&I School

Horseshoe

(Based on Carol Ann Duffy 'Valentine')

Not a red rose or a satin heart,
I give you a horseshoe painted red.
It promises good luck,
Here.
It will brighten up your room,
It will make your heart a-flutter.
I am trying to be romantic,
Not a joker, or a nutter.

Not a cute card, or kissogram,
I give you a horseshoe painted red.
It promises a smile,
Here.
It will cheer you up,
It will make your day.
I'm trying to be loving,
Not mean or scare you away.

Amelia Carter (10)
St Chad's CE Primary School, Brighouse

A Red Ring

(Based on Carol Ann Duffy 'Valentine')

Not a rose or a satin heart.
I give you a red ring.
It promises every time I'm with you
There will always be a full moon.

Benedict Barron (10)
St Chad's CE Primary School, Brighouse

Love Me

(Based on Carol Ann Duffy 'Valentine')

Not a rose or a satin heart
I give you a tomato
It promises love and enjoyment
Here
It will show you the path of love.
It will give you enjoyment of love.
I am trying to be loyal
Not a cheat or a liar.
I will love you till the death.
Nothing could break my love
Only you.

Emma Baldwin (10)
St Chad's CE Primary School, Brighouse

Valentine Or Moped?

(Based on Carol Ann Duffy 'Valentine')

Not a rose or a satin heart.
I give you a moped
It promises speed and agility.
Here,
It will whizz you through traffic,
It will get you to me!
I am trying to be helpful.
Not a cute card or kissogram,
A moped with love from me to you.

Ryan Sharp (9)
St Chad's CE Primary School, Brighouse

Johnny Mill

Johnny Mill,
Johnny Mill,
Ate a giant shiny pill.

Shiny pill,
Shiny pill,
Then went to a big, big mill.

Big, big mill,
Big, big mill,
Then grew a colourful gill.

Colourful gill,
Colourful gill,
And he got very ill.

George Pearson (9)
St Chad's CE Primary School, Brighouse

Mathilda Lee

Mathilda Lee,
Mathilda Lee,
Ate baked beans for her tea

For her tea,
For her tea,
Went unconscious and couldn't see!

Conor Durkin (9)
St Chad's CE Primary School, Brighouse

I Hope You Like It

(Based on Carol Ann Duffy 'Valentine')

Not a rose or a satin heart,
I give you a pebble.
It promises mystery,
Here.
It will always stay with you,
It will never die.
I am trying to be honest,
Not a novelty or a box of chocolates,
I give you a pebble,
Its smoothness will please you,
Strong and everlasting as we are,
For as long as we are.
Take it,
Solid as a rock,
If you like
Unbreakable,
Its beauty will never change,
Its colour will never fade.

Victoria Pearson (9)
St Chad's CE Primary School, Brighouse

Candle

(Based on Carol Ann Duffy 'Valentine')

Not a red rose or satin heart.
I give you a candle
It will always shine.
It will never run out,
Like the gleaming light of love.
Not a red rose or satin heart.

Daniel Burnside (9)
St Chad's CE Primary School, Brighouse

The Cappuccino Of Love

(Based on Carol Ann Duffy 'Valentine')

Not a rose or satin heart,
I give you a cappuccino,
It is a muddy pool of love,
It promises caffeine to give you a buzz,
Like putting your finger in an electric socket.

Here.
You can drink it with pleasure,
It will remind you of me,
It will be as sweet as love's first kiss.
I am trying to be caring
I will not be a liar,
This is not a joke.
Its hot burning power will slide down your throat,
This advice is meant to be helpful,
Not worrying or tiring.

I give you a cappuccino,
It's especially from me.
xxx

Bethany Dimmock (10)
St Chad's CE Primary School, Brighouse

Love Is A TV Clicker

(Based on Carol Ann Duffy 'Valentine')

Not a rose or a satin heart,
I give you a TV clicker,
It promises to keep my love switched on,
It will always channel my affection to you,
It will never go on standby,
I am trying to be on the same wavelength,
Not a cuddly teddy or a box of chocolates.

Victoria Wetton (10)
St Chad's CE Primary School, Brighouse

The Deadly, Dopey Dog

The deadly, dopey dog is as fierce as a pack of wolves
(All) As fierce as a pack of wolves
(Solo) As fierce as a pack of wolves.

The deadly, dopey dog is as dopey as a goldfish,
(All) As dopey as a goldfish,
(Solo) As dopey as a goldfish.

The deadly, dopey dog wouldn't know if he was eating from
a mouldy dish,
(All) He wouldn't know if he was eating from a mouldy dish,
(Solo) He wouldn't know if he was eating from a mouldy dish.

The deadly, dopey dog goes to Colombia every year,
(All) Goes to Colombia every year,
(Solo) Goes to Colombia every year.

The deadly, dopey dog drinks a bottle of beer
(All) Drinks a bottle of beer
(Solo) Drinks a bottle of beer.

The deadly, dopey dog has a midday doze
(All) Has a midday doze
(Solo) Has a midday doze.

Jessica Hagain (9)
St Chad's CE Primary School, Brighouse

Love Poems

(Based on Carol Ann Duffy 'Valentine')

My heart is like a red, red rose
That's newly sprung in June.
My love is like a melody that plays a sweet tune.
And when my brain looks at you it thinks, *hobba, hobba*
She is loving, caring, respectful, helpful, kind, thoughtful, honest,
sharing person.

Andrew Maycock (10)
St Chad's CE Primary School, Brighouse

The Fearsome St Chad's School Monster

The fearsome St Chad's School monster has muscles the size
of a greenhouse.

Has muscles the size of a greenhouse.
Muscles the size of a greenhouse . . .

The fearsome St Chad's School monster has a brain the size
of a pea.

A brain the size of a pea.
Brain the size of a pea . . .

The fearsome St Chad's School monster is as tall as skyscrapers
in New York.

As tall as skyscrapers in New York.
As tall as skyscrapers in New York . . .

The fearsome St Chad's School monster has hair as ratty
as bear trees.

Has hair as ratty as bear trees.
Has hair as ratty as bear trees . . .

Peter Walker (10)
St Chad's CE Primary School, Brighouse

Red Ball

(Based on Carol Ann Duffy 'Valentine')

Not a red rose or a satin heart
I give you a red ball.
It promises to always bounce back to you like my love.
Here.
It will warm your heart with its red glow.
It will be like my love, a never-ending circle.
I am trying to be honest
Not a flower that will die or a chocolate heart that will melt.
But a big red ball, to keep for life.

Lewis Reid (9)
St Chad's CE Primary School, Brighouse

Hilda King

Hilda King,
Hilda King,
Had a pretty diamond ring.
Diamond ring,
Diamond ring,
Made Hilda want to sing.
Want to sing,
Want to sing,
Except for when the doorbell rings.
Doorbell rings,
Doorbell rings,
Someone with some earrings.
Earrings,
Earrings,
To match her pretty diamond ring.

Jamie Shackleton (9)
St Chad's CE Primary School, Brighouse

Red Circle

(Based on Carol Ann Duffy 'Valentine')

Not a rose or a satin heart
It promises love
Here.
It will comfort you
It will remind you of me
I am trying to be loving
Not a square or a triangle
But a red circle,
And a circle is the shape of a wedding ring
My eternal love for you
And my passionate love for you
My never-ending love.

Bradley Seymour (9)
St Chad's CE Primary School, Brighouse

Carrot

(Based on Carol Ann Duffy 'Valentine')

Not a rose or satin heart.
I give you a carrot,
It promises light
Here.
It will keep you safe,
It will be a light of yours.
I am trying to be kind,
Not a dark night or black sight.

I give you a carrot.
Its glow will last forever,
Safe and light
As you are,
For as long as you are.

Take it, its shining light blinds the unsafe,
If you like
Lethal
Its light will stay in your eyes,
Cling to the glow.
Lethal.

Nicole Riach (10)
St Chad's CE Primary School, Brighouse

A Tomato

(Based on Carol Ann Duffy 'Valentine')

Not a rose or a satin heart
I give you a tomato
It promises seeds of love
Here
It will grow love
Between us
It will keep us together forever
I am trying to be sincere
Not a fool or an idiot.

Nathaniel Leah (9)
St Chad's CE Primary School, Brighouse

Mathilda Lee

Mathilda Lee,
Mathilda Lee,
Ate baked beans for her tea.

For her tea,
For her tea,
Went unconscious and couldn't see.

Barry Lane,
Barry Lane,
For breakfast he had wholegrain.

Had wholegrain,
Had wholegrain,
Because he had a tummy pain.

A tummy pain,
A tummy pain,
Because he ate wholegrain.

Beth Adamson (9)
St Chad's CE Primary School, Brighouse

Not A Rose Or A Satin Heart

(Based on Carol Ann Duffy 'Valentine')

Not a rose or a satin heart
I give you a tomato
It promises to be sweet
Here.
It will make your heart burst with its sweetness
It will grind your teeth with its seeds of love.
I am trying to be loving
Not a box of chocolates or a hug.
I give you a tomato.
And it will fill you with goodness.

Luke Baranyai (9)
St Chad's CE Primary School, Brighouse

I Give You

(Based on Carol Ann Duffy 'Valentine')

Not a rose or a satin heart,
I give you an apple,
It promises a good, healthy life.
Here.
It will grow,
It will strengthen our love,
I am trying to be honest.
Not a box of chocolates or a teddy.
I give you an apple.
Its sweet taste will remind you of me,
Cute and kissable.
For as long as
Our friendship grows,
Share it
And just leave seeds,
If you like.
Not to be eaten,
Its taste will be hard to your bite,
But soft in your mouth.

Kirsty Monday (10)
St Chad's CE Primary School, Brighouse

Twinkle Little Goat

(Inspired by 'Twinkle, Twinkle Little Star')

Twinkle, twinkle little goat
With your warm and furry coat
Eating grass all day long
Don't eat books 'cause that is *wrong!*

Connor Trevelyan & Adam Cockayne (8)
St Helen's CE Aided J&I School, Pontefract

Auntie Mabel

(Inspired by 'Twinkle, Twinkle Little Star')

Twinkle, twinkle little ghost
Have you eaten all my toast?
A minute ago it was on the table
Or could it have been my auntie Mabel?

**Joshua Conway, Nathan Cargill, Connor Trevelyan,
Jonathan Deaville, Kieran Olbison, Curtis Petch & Jay Cook**
St Helen's CE Aided J&I School, Pontefract

David Plane

David Plane is a pain
He makes people disappear
First you're gone
Then you're here
We don't know where you came from!

Aidan Garrett & Jonathan Deaville (7)
St Helen's CE Aided J&I School, Pontefract

Harry Latt

Harry Latt is a giant bat.
His wings are black.
His eyes are big.
He gets a smack.
When he eats like a pig.

Year 3 (8)
St Helen's CE Aided J&I School, Pontefract

Twinkle Little Witch

(Inspired by 'Twinkle, Twinkle Little Star')

Twinkle, twinkle little witch,
Casting spells to make kids itch.
Flying on your broom all day
You like to get your own way.

Year 3 (8)
St Helen's CE Aided J&I School, Pontefract

Bernard Bunny

Bernard Bunny
Is rather funny.
His hands are made of jelly.
His ears are dark green.
He has a big fat belly.
He is a soldier for the queen.

**Jack Hiley, Liam Goodlad, Shauna Mee, Katy Skidmore,
Olivia Dickens & Joshua Ryan (8)**
St Helen's CE Aided J&I School, Pontefract

The Wild Sea

In the wild sea some little fish were swimming
Swimming into the Weston Sea
There were some strange objects.
There was a flag
And an old fishing rod
And it started to float away
Crash!

Simon Bottomley (9)
St John's CE (A) J&I School, Golcar

Storm

A twirling twister ripping across the land,
Lightning flashes, thunder booms and the sea crashes
in a swirling frenzy.
Rain belts down like stone.
Volcano fires blaze into ashes on the ground.
Children cry,
Mothers scream and fathers yell in the packed bomb shelter.
Vicars pray and beggars crouch in corners with their arms
over their heads.
Roads overflow, carts crash down lanes and streets.
People drown.
Tornados twist and turn in an angry fury.
Volcanoes burst into life after hundreds of years of peace.
Earthquakes rumble all over the world,
Cows stampede for some dry shelter.
Horses gallop through the terror-filled town.
Fire engines and ambulances roam the streets and roads.
Sirens screech and squeal into life all over the city.
Cars crash and lorries tip.
Roofs collapse into houses while people worry.
Hurricanes blast through buildings.
Tidal waves crash over once beautiful sandy beaches.
Wendy houses crash through the cities.
Walls blow through.
Windows smash into people's faces.

At last all that is left of the towns and cities and villages is wreckage,
ruin and death.
Babies cry as people look at what was once their homes.

Nat Gregory (9)
St John's CE (A) J&I School, Golcar

Ten Different Ways The Weather Is Like A Person Or An Animal

The sun is like a newborn baby.
The rain is like a cup dropped from a high surface.
The thunder is like a tiger roaring.
The flashing lightning is like a light bulb.
The stars' twinkle is like an eye of a unicorn.
The wind is like a giraffe in a mood.
An earthquake is like an elephant's stamp.
The sunset is like a panda eating.
The sunrise is like somebody falling out of bed.
The tornado is like a ballerina spinning.

Megan Woods (10)
St John's CE (A) J&I School, Golcar

The Horror

Like a nuclear bomb dropping from the sky.
Ker-splash! It pierces the ground
It is a raindrop!
Its brother is coming up from the depths
Like a water viper ready to strike.
Pop! It reaches the surface;
It is an air bubble!

Alex Jones (9)
St John's CE (A) J&I School, Golcar

Red Racer!

Shiny, glossy Ferrari zooming down the road
Rushing at high speeds.
Sixty miles per hour maybe?
May have been going faster
Bumping, crashing, flying over the hillsides rapidly,
Unstoppably fast, speeding down the road.
Hoping not to meet anything at the other end.
Shaking terribly while feeding more accelerator by the minute.
Bang, bash, boom, wallop, he's crashed the car!
Smoke everywhere, bits of red Ferrari flying everywhere.
Red-hot flames gushing up to the sky,
Roaring around the street, black instant smoke
Prowling within the clouds, booming out of the engine.
The truck he crashed into was even worse.
It was in bite-size pieces big enough for a mouse!

Jack Midwood (9)
St John's CE (A) J&I School, Golcar

Flower Fairies

Flower fairies live in the deepest, longest forests,
They say the forest is enchanted with fairies
And they live in little roses, little red roses.
All day they sleep in their tiny, tiny beds and only wake at night.
They play all night with other creatures
And they listen for any sign of danger.
So, what mischievous things do they get up to?
They put spells on people and do lots of other things too.
When they get tired, they go home and rest,
They drift off to sleep to start another day.
Look out for fairies
You don't know
What they can
Do!

Eleanor Smith (9)
St John's CE (A) J&I School, Golcar

The Mythical Monster

Eyes glistened in the sun
Nose as big as the Atlantic Ocean
Mouth as jagged as a bush, all surrounded by a hideous face.
Belly, bubbly, bouncy and very fat.
The sounds his belly makes are indescribable
And they could deafen you.
Arms made out of springs' rusty metal.
He can never hold anything still.
Legs as thin as sticks, they can barely hold him up
He's forever falling over.
Hands and feet are multicoloured,
They look like they have got hand gloves on and foot gloves on.
Toes are dreadful and slimy.
The gorgon.

Sarah Nixon (10)
St John's CE (A) J&I School, Golcar

As Sly As A Fox

Deep down into the deep dark forest lurks a wolf as sly as a fox.
Every night he comes out to catch his prey then howls,
Howls in the moonlight like a singing lark.
He catches his prey with pride.
He runs as fast as the tide.
His coat is dark, dark, dark.
He climbs the trees slyly;
It has been a long day for the wolf as sly as a fox.
In his barn there he lay, sound asleep in the hay.

Grace Young-Roberts (9)
St John's CE (A) J&I School, Golcar

Windy Days

It's still winter,
Very cold trees with no leaves,
Grass still soggy but green,
Everybody falling in the mud,
Boys skidding in the mud,
Girls playing girly games,
Adults working,
People catching colds,
Sun trying to shine,
Grey, dark clouds.
Teachers, teaching,
Children working.
Tornados gushing around,
Wind blowing,
Thud!
People falling over,
Hats blowing off people's heads,
Dogs blowing everywhere,
Flower pots falling,
The sea gushing back into streams and rivers.

Melissa Whitwam (10)
St John's CE (A) J&I School, Golcar

The Fire Monster

Fire, fire, the fire monster is burning down buildings,
Burning down homes.
Water is rushing left and right.
He was flying up and down
People going down the road
Monster going home to bed.

Connor Fawcett (9)
St John's CE (A) J&I School, Golcar

Mystery Monster

Mysteriously multicoloured
This murderous monster murmured soundlessly asleep.
Scaly and bloodthirsty he jolted awake.
This repulsive dragon.
He rode ravenously mid-flight looking for humans to feast on,
He soared among the hilltops and scampered through the glen
And then, after a while, he went home again.
After a century this dangerous dragon died.
There's no more murderous, multicoloured creature
Soaring across the sky,
But the dragon's secret will never be revealed,
For everybody's lips are now sealed.
Now where the dragon is laid underground,
He will not be slain ever again.

Annie Shaw (10)
St John's CE (A) J&I School, Golcar

Waiting For You To Grow

Sunflower, sunflower waiting for you to grow
I will give you light, I will give you soil, I will let the rain fall.
Sunflower, sunflower, waiting for you to grow
I will give you a beautiful colour yellow, bright yellow.
Sunflower, sunflower waiting for you to grow
I will give you leaves the colour of green, yes light green.
When the snow falls I will keep you safe in a garage.
There will be light; there will be water, safe and sound.
Sunflower, sunflower you are dying, dying.
Sunflower, sunflower in summer you are growing, growing, growing.
The sun has come again the bright light
You are free again, you are free
I will give you water, soil and light.

Jack Lockwood (9)
St John's CE (A) J&I School, Golcar

The Big Sun

The sun is hot.
The sun is hot.
The sun is hot because you are happy.
The sun is big.
The sun is full of sweets.
When the sun goes down you are sad.
We all love the sun.
But when we wake up the sun is up too.
The sun is like a big jacuzzi to sit in.
The sun is hot.
The sun is hot.
The sun is in with the planets.
The sun is like a football in the air.
The sun shines on the garden every day.
The sun is hot.
The sun is hot.
The sun is very, very hot.
But in winter the sun goes away to his bed.
But I am happy in summer when it is out again.
The sun is hot.
The sun is fun.
The sun is like a fairground.
The sun shines on the treetops.

Charlotte Fox (9)
St John's CE (A) J&I School, Golcar

Scary Man

Woo, woo in the night I saw a scary man.
He had scars like a tree and he floats like a leaf falling to the ground.
His blazing eyes turn you to smoke.

Reece Sykes (10)
St John's CE (A) J&I School, Golcar

Outside

Trees waving
Side to side
Back and forward
Leaves dropping
Blue clouds slowly flowing
Muddy floors
Green grass
Big trees
A gorgeous breeze
The sky peeking
Big tall mills
White goalposts
Green hills
Loads of
Tall built houses.

Joshua Woods (9)
St John's CE (A) J&I School, Golcar

One Day I Saw A Monster

One day I saw a monster
With massive sharp claws
And a massive scaly back
And its ginormous eyes
Its teeth all rotten
And its fiery breath
And its massive ginormous feet.

Nathan Firth (9)
St John's CE (A) J&I School, Golcar

My Spell

A drop of joy,
A magic hat
And a dancing rabbit.

The sun that glistens in the sky,
A laugh from a gang of friends
And the smell of lavender.

A wizard of wisdom,
Some magic beans
And a frog's leg that's still moving.

A land of dreams,
A mean nasty monster
And one strip of lightning.

A galloping pony in a muddy field
A spiky rose bush
And a charming, still stream.

Hot steaming lava from a volcano
A glisten from a midnight horse
And that's my spell.

Molly Ashmore (10)
St John's CE (A) J&I School, Golcar

Caterpillar

Caterpillar, caterpillar where are you?
Caterpillar crawls into a shoe
Caterpillars are very hairy
Caterpillar aren't at all like fairies
Leaves you eat
You don't like meat
You crawl up the tree and go into a cocoon
You break up and evolve into a butterfly with wings like a rainbow.

Laura Mallalieu   (9)
St John's CE (A) J&I School, Golcar

The Magic Box

(Based on 'Magic Box' by Kit Wright)

I will put in my box . . .
An owl of kindness
A candle of happiness
A key of excitement
A book full of warmth

I will put in my box . . .
A snowflake as magical as a unicorn
A necklace of fashion
A roar of a lion
A smile from a baby
A voice of a rabbit

My box is covered with books
It stands on heads
And it's got a lock shaped
Like an owl.

Haydn Todd (10)
St John's CE (A) J&I School, Golcar

The Thing

Something falling from the sky.
Faster and faster that thing is still falling.
It seems to never touch the ground.
It seems to be floating.
What is it?
It looks like a star.
It's coming this way . . .
Is it a snowflake?
Yes!

Callum Peel (9)
St John's CE (A) J&I School, Golcar

Friends

My friends came round one night,
The best part was the pillow fight!

We will draw everything in the colour red,
So we will never ever go to bed.

We will all wake up with a yawn,
At the sight of the amazing dawn.

We will all get up and get dressed,
We will hope that we look our best.

Then we will all go to the mall,
I will have to bring my special teddy that's really small.

But sadly my friends have to go,
They leave me playing with my magic bow.

Limara Gay (10)
St John's CE (A) J&I School, Golcar

When I Went Out For A Walk One Day

When I went out for a walk one day
My head fell off and rolled away,
And when I saw that it was gone
I picked it up and put it back on.

I went down the street one day
Someone shouted look at your feet.
I looked at them and sadly said,
'I've left them both asleep in bed.'

Harry Hutchinson (9)
St John's CE (A) J&I School, Golcar

The Man

There once was a man that was blind,
He really did need to unwind.
He got a big cut, right on his butt,
Then he wasn't that very much kind.

The man was very rich,
He could afford a football pitch.
Nobody could care less,
Apart from his sister Bess.

She wasn't the best of people,
Knocked off the church's steeple.
An Afro lay on her head,
Next thing you know her brother is dead!

He rose up high to the heavens,
And did his timetables, his last were his sevens.
Now I have to come to an end
With this poem, please do send.

Callum Mair (10)
St John's CE (A) J&I School, Golcar

The Dragon

The dragon strongly snorts a puff
The dragon blows a flame
The dragon burns down buildings
The dragon turns the blue river to steam
The dragon hides inside a cave where no one can see
The mother dragon's little baby buzzing like a bee.

Leigh-Amy Ruff (10)
St John's CE (A) J&I School, Golcar

The Three-Headed Monster

This three-headed monster walks to me.
Its eyes glow in my face.
The light it blinds and it burns me.
With its seventeen claws, it scares me.
Its curly hair is revolting!
As its six arms and hands try to strangle me.
So I get out my sword and chop off its head
As it rolls further, further towards me.
His five legs are left standing as his head rolls off the cliff!

Darcy Edgar (9)
St John's CE (A) J&I School, Golcar

Windy Night

The stars were shining brightly until a bolt of lightning struck.
Pow, pow, pow!
The world was shaking side to side.
It was like a volcano pushing out the hot steamy lava.
It rained for two nights and the rain was like snowdrops and splashed
one by one.
Thunder crashing like a bunny hopping about
Thump, thump, thump!
The third day the sun was out and the kids were in the sun.

Katie O'Brien (9)
St John's CE (A) J&I School, Golcar

My Fairy

My fairy is a little girl, she has tiny wings.
In the sky my fairy flies up and down incessantly.
My fairy is a good girl at heart, but a bad girl on the outside.
She lives in a teeny box and she sleeps in an undersized bed.

Victoria Atkinson (10)
St John's CE (A) J&I School, Golcar

Flowers

Flowers, flowers, fluttering flowers all on a windy day
There are daffodils, daisies and roses too
They blossom all around just for you
But when I close my eyes they only disappear
When I open my eyes there are flowers everywhere
Flowers come, flowers go, but they normally stay until the snow
When they come it's so fun picking them for display.

Chelsea Redshaw (9)
St John's CE (A) J&I School, Golcar

Silence

It was as silent as a kitten climbing a tree.
It was as silent as a bird gliding in the sky.
It was as silent as a crocodile in the water.
It was as silent as a hedgehog scurrying across the road.
It was as silent as a squirrel running up a tree.
It was as silent as a mouse running into its nest.
It was as silent as a peacock spreading its feathers.
It was as silent as a giraffe walking in the grass.
It was as silent as a tiger eating its prey.

Matthew Bramham (8)
St Patrick's Primary School, Birstall

Treasure Box

My treasure box is one of the most important things I have got.
When it is a fairy day I go up to my room,
Close my door and then I get my treasure box out.
I sit on my bed, open my treasure box
And get out some thread, small paints, a brush and some beads.
Then paint my thread and put some beads on and make a necklace.

Fay Brown (8)
St Patrick's Primary School, Birstall

Silence

As silent as a cat running along the path.
A fish paddling and diving.
A snail slithering in the snow.
A cloud.
A frog jumping across the snow.
A squirrel climbing up a tree.
A teardrop running down the poor boy's face.
A girl's hair brushing her shoulders.
A leaf falling from a tree.
A dog moving in the snow.
A little nail dropping on the grass.
A piece of grass dropping to the ground.
A piece of paper falling on the snow.
A mouse running across the grass.
The sounds of silence.

Mia Green (7)
St Patrick's Primary School, Birstall

Giant

If I was a big giant
I would see everything.
I would see a busy town.
I would see green fields and the beautiful blue sea.
I would lift things up and look over hills.
I'd have a big stamp!
I would be so tall.
I would be so strong.
I would lift incredible things up.
I would have tough hands.
I would have tough shoulders.

Connor Butterfield (7)
St Patrick's Primary School, Birstall

Sweets

S weets are my favourite
W ine gums are ace
E at more sweets
E veryone likes sweets
T errific sweets
S weets yum! Yum! Yum!

Bradley Flavell (8)
St Patrick's Primary School, Birstall

Wings

If I had wings I would swoop like an eagle.
I would dive like a fish.
I would glide like a seagull.
I would hover like a hawk.
I would rise like a cloud.
I would soar like a dragonfly.

Patrick Flowers (7)
St Patrick's Primary School, Birstall

Stars

S hiny stars
H ooray it is shiny
I am a star
N ew shiny star
Y es I like that star.

Joseph Foster (7)
St Patrick's Primary School, Birstall

If I Were A Peacock

If I were a peacock I would have a beautiful feathery tail.
Its colours would be . . .
As blue as the sky
As green as the grass
As red as the rose
As black as the pig
As yellow as the sun
As grey as the elephant
As beautiful as a stallion.

Holly Speight (8)
St Patrick's Primary School, Birstall

Days Of The Week

On Monday I fell off my bike.
On Tuesday I grazed my knee.
On Wednesday I fell down the steps.
On Thursday I broke my neck.
On Friday a dog bit my shin.
On Saturday I lost my best toy.
On Sunday I slept in bed.
After those days I've just had . . .
Everything was boring.

Olivia Hilton (8)
St Patrick's Primary School, Birstall

Whale

W hales are big.
H owling at sharks.
A lways with each other.
L oves water.
E ats fish.

Kieran Goodman (8)
St Patrick's Primary School, Birstall

Can You See?

Can you see a door opening?
Can you see a baby walking?
Can you see a mouse rolling?
Can you see a bird swooping?
Can you see a cheetah running?
Can you see a frog leaping?
Can you see a spider crawling?
Can you see a rhino charging?
Look at all the animals that can do things,
So amazing!

George O'Hara (7)
St Patrick's Primary School, Birstall

Gentle

It was as gentle as a bug.
It was as gentle as a butterfly moving in the air.
It was as gentle as a moth hiding in the light.
It was as gentle as a leaf flowing in the wind.
It was as gentle as the raindrops dropping one by one.
It was as gentle as the wind blowing in the trees.
It was as gentle as a mouse scurrying across the floor.
It was as gentle as a fish swimming in the sea.

Nathan Jones (7)
St Patrick's Primary School, Birstall

Stars

S tars are bright.
T hey shine over me
A nd my house.
R ight over everywhere.

Siobhan Orange (7)
St Patrick's Primary School, Birstall

If I Was A Hedgehog

If I was a hedgehog I could rustle in the leaves.
If I was a hedgehog I could munch my food.
If I was a hedgehog I would hibernate in the winter in
                                    a cosy warm nest.
If I was a hedgehog I would get up in the night and scurry across
                                    the path in the moonlight.
If I was a hedgehog I would wander wherever I liked.
I wouldn't make any noise at all.
If I was a hedgehog I would love it.

Laura Russell (7)
St Patrick's Primary School, Birstall

Playful

As playful as a dog.
As a horse running in the field.
As a squirrel scuttling in the tree and searching for nuts.
As a butterfly flapping his wings.
As worms wiggling along the ground.
As the trees swaying along the breeze.
As the birds swooping along the floor.
Do you like animals?

Nadiah Kazzan (8)
St Patrick's Primary School, Birstall

Friends

N ever annoys you.
A lways gets on with her work.
D oes her work in silence.
I am her best friend.
A lways does funny things.
H as two dogs, Nala and Lulu.

Chantel Morris (8)
St Patrick's Primary School, Birstall

Crocodile

C rocodile
R oars like a monster
O n the surface of the river.
C atches fish for tea.
O h how terrifying he looks!
D oes all his work smiling.
I n the reeds he hurts.
L ikes to eat teachers!
E ats them all up!

Conor Harrington (7)
St Patrick's Primary School, Birstall

Connor

C onnor is my friend.
O ver a mountain.
N ot a worry.
N ever naughty.
O r a great football player.
R eally good at rugby.

Max Senior (7)
St Patrick's Primary School, Birstall

Cats

C ats are good pets.
A cat is soft and furry.
T hey are clever.
S hiny eyes at night.

Hannah Senior (7)
St Patrick's Primary School, Birstall

Trees

T rees can sway from side to side.
R ed leaves fall from the tree to the ground.
E very year the leaves fall in winter.
E very day leaves fall in winter.
S ometimes they change colour.

Chloe Barrett (7)
St Patrick's Primary School, Birstall

Shark

S cary
H as fins
A ttacks fish
R ips its prey
K ills easily.

Patrick Sykes (8)
St Patrick's Primary School, Birstall

Tom

T antrum king of all.
O ld and grumpy.
M ean and vicious.

Tom Bottomley (7)
St Patrick's Primary School, Birstall

Dads

D ads love you
A dad would kiss you
D ads put you to sleep
S itting about, then they go to sleep.

Alex Burnett (8)
St Patrick's Primary School, Birstall

Bunnies

Bunnies are cute
Bunnies hop around
Bunnies hop up and down
Bunnies are fun
Bunnies are great
Bunnies hop around
Up and down and over the gate
Bunnies are good for you
They like to hop with you.

Sinead White (9)
Sutton-In-Craven CP School

The Racers

Racers race
But keep up the pace,
Racers rock
But have a great big
Shock!
When they
Crash!

Joshua Wood (9)
Sutton-In-Craven CP School

Spring

S pring smells like chocolate.
P repare for new birth,
R epresents new life,
I ndeed there will be rain
N ever dying things
G rowing and everlasting birth.

I nsects come out and scurry about,
S inging little sparrows.

L ambs run with care,
O range and purple crocuses,
V ery comforting.
I rises peek their heads.
N ever miss out on spring,
G rowing and everlasting birth.

Tanya Hunter (11)
Sutton-In-Craven CP School

Summer

S ummer is a bright time to play
U sing a bucket and spade on the beach
M int ice cream on the floor
M um is shouting, 'Sit down the barbecue is ready.'
E verybody is listening to birds in the trees
R ight it is eight o'clock, time for bed.
Summer!

Becky Simpson (10)
Sutton-In-Craven CP School

Choco Chocolate

Choco chocolate melts in your mouth,
It's warm and fuzzy and it makes you shout.
It's creamy, dark, milk and plain,
But I love it all the same.
It shows desire and affection
And it's yummy did I mention!

Kayleigh Davies (11)
Sutton-In-Craven CP School

Football

Football is fun, football is great
Just for football, you'd come rushing out your gate!
Man United is the best team
For Man United you'd give a great scream.
Without football there would be nothing to do
For football is the best thing for you!

Leah Thompson (9)
Sutton-In-Craven CP School

Drama

Drama is the joy of life,
It helps me with my fears and frights.
In bed at night it helps me think of all the things only fluffy and pink.
I act, I sing, I dance all night, dancing to the music, oh what a sight.

Braidi Woods (10)
Sutton-In-Craven CP School

Watch Out For The Dirty House On The Hill

The robot dog
In the living room sleeping
Though when it awakes
You'll wish you were dreaming.

If you ever step into the house for a dare
You'll be sure to be tearing out your hair!

The blood on the floor will
Drown you to death
There's no use shouting
As you breathe your last breath,
The kitchen floor
All littered with bones
I walked to the fridge
All alone.

If you ever step into the house for a dare
You'll be sure to be tearing out your hair!

The big black bear rug
Gives you a bear hug
Before squeezing you into its mouth *glug!*
The black and white teeth on the piano
Just like my grandma's
Long ago.

If you enter the house on the hill for a dare
You'll be sure to be tearing out your hair!

Jessica Clegg (10)
Wakefield Tutorial School

World Seasons

When spring comes and starts you see . . .
Leaping lambs jumping
Shining sun shining
Blooming buds bursting
And brand new turned leaves.

When summer then rules you see . . .
Cool ice cream melting
Summer sun scorching
Sweet straw hats cooling
And summer fruit puds.

Autumn creeps in and you see . . .
Lush leaves fall softly
Fungus flocks thriving
Harvest moon rising
And departing ducks.

When winter frost comes you see . . .
Darker days looming
Santa's sleigh flying
Friendly fires warming
And perfect pressies.

Felicia Doubell (11)
Wakefield Tutorial School

Alphabet Poem

Apples in the tree
Bananas are yellow
Cats are furry
Dogs rolling in the mud
Elephants spraying water
Fox eyes glowing in the dark
Giraffes with long necks
Hedgehogs are brown
Ice creams are cold
Jacob is a name
Kay gives us a lift to school
Lauren is my friend
Mohammed likes monkeys
Nikos is a boy
Octopus' have eight legs
Pandas are animals
Quack goes the duck
Rabbits are cute
Snakes are fast
The train is a transport
Umbrellas are used in a storm
Vixen is a flying reindeer
Water is what we drink
Xylophones are musical instruments
Yachts are boats with sails
Zebra is the name of an animal.

Jacob Atkinson (9)
Wakefield Tutorial School

Autumn

Hedgehogs hibernate
Harvest moon
Flame red
Ripe wheat
Warm, crisp moon
Deep, purple flush
Many birds may leave
Days getting shorter
Crisp darker nights
Speckled leaves, mottled leaves
Bruised leaves, clumped leaves
Red, yellow, brown leaves
Crunching all night.

Imogen Wade (9)
Wakefield Tutorial School

Trees In Winter

Holly is an evergreen
It dances like a fairy queen
Fir trees sway in the breeze
Even fires start to freeze
Snowdrops fall from the sky
This is when some trees die
Robins start to build their nests
The twigs and moss are always the best
Winter's the opposite of July
In this weather you will never find a butterfly.

Holly Taylor-Whitehead (9)
Wakefield Tutorial School

Flowers

I love bluebells
Lovely shiny blue
Blowing in the summer wind
Especially for you.

Orchids opening at the beginning of spring
Bees taking pollen
Falling onto their wings.

Tulips turning round and round
Lovely as they are
I can hear them singing
Which is a lovely sound.

Snowdrops on the ground, lovely and white
When it becomes to the end
Of the day it is night-time
Sleep tight.

Daffodils dancing in
The moonlight and all the
Flowers are singing and
Prancing.

I love all flowers.

Holly Latham (9)
Wakefield Tutorial School

Ten Of Everything

Ten robots crushing,
One got crushed, then there were nine.
Nine freaky frogs,
One melted, then there were eight.
Eight racing cars,
One burst his tyre, then there were seven.
Seven slimy slugs,
One got lost, then there were six.
Six pufferfish,
One got puffed out and then there were five.
Five freezing fingers,
One got frostbite, and then there were four.
Four pencil marks.
One got rubbed out, then there were three.
Three snowmen in the garden,
One melted away, then there were two.
Two naughty school boys,
One ran away, then there was one,
One guitar,
Broke its strings, then that was
The end!

Joseph Elliott (9)
Wakefield Tutorial School

On The Farm

In the pigsty
The pigs
Pant and puff.

In the stable
The horses
Neigh and nod.

In the cowshed
The cows
Sniff and snort.

In the shed
The tractor
Lifts and loads.

In the farmhouse
My mum's
Cooking and cleaning.

In the farmyard
The people
Brush and build.

In the field
The sheep
Frolic with frenzy.

James Rathmell (8)
Wakefield Tutorial School

Night-Time

Night-time is scary time!
Was the door creaking my imagination?
Or did I really see something - a ghost looking at me?
The wind is howling and roaring loudly.
Why can't I sleep so soundly?
The steps are squeaking now, the taps are leaking.
Then you think it is all quiet, but then
You hear the rain pouring down in a riot,
Splashing on the windowpane.
Crash comes the thunder and the lightning!
You lie there listening forever.
Then the clock in the hall gives a loud clang!
You toss and turn feeling hot and cold
Trying to remember what you have been told
There's nothing to worry about!

Anna Sheldon (9)
Wakefield Tutorial School

In The Winter

In the winter it is always
Breezy.
Everyone rides on their sledges.
It is really freezing
In the winter snow.

In the winter
You will need a scarf
Or else you will freeze to death.
Everything is wrapped up in a snow blanket.
Even the tree barks are white
In the cold, cold winter snow.

George Judd (8)
Wakefield Tutorial School

In The Garden

In the garden there are
Lilies lilting,
Lupins lurching,
Roses raving,
Rhododendrons rocking,
Trees twisting in the breeze,
Sweet-smelling snowdrops swaying softly,
Crocuses curtsying in the sunshine,
On the fence is an orchard.

Now the winter's here everything is dead.
Now there are no lilies lilting,
Lupins lurching,
Roses raving,
No rhododendrons rocking,
No trees twisting,
No sweet-smelling snowdrops,
No crocuses curtsying,
Not even a flower
Until the springtime comes.

Amy Cassar (8)
Wakefield Tutorial School

Winter

In the winter I wrap up warm
Sitting by the fire till the crack of dawn
I have a hot chocolate and go to bed
I don't go to sleep I watch TV instead.

In the morning I have a lie in
I go down to breakfast and get stuck in the bin
I go outside and build a snowman
I call over my dad and he helps all he can.

It's just gone past Christmas time
People come round and sang and said a rhyme
I like having a snowball fight
My friends could do it all through the night.

Snow is cold and also white
It really sparkles through the night
I like snow it is so fun
It is fun for everyone.

Charlotte Alton (9)
Westville House School

Pets

My pet is a cat
Who sleeps on a mat
And also he is very fat.

My pet is a dog
Who sleeps on a log
And his name's Mog.

My pet is a fish
And he lives in a dish
And he always makes a wish.

My pet is a rabbit
Who has a bad habit
Give him a carrot and he will grab it.

Ellen Dewhurst (8)
Westville House School

Seasons

Autumn is great
There are so many leaves
Play hide-and-seek
And hide in the leaves.

Winter is cool
You have snowball fights
Snow is the best
Come and play.

Spring is great
We have a lot of fun
You see baby
Lambs and calves.

Summer is hot
Like a hot microwave
Summer is a time
To play with your friends.

Kodie Brook (8)
Westville House School

I Wish I Had Fairy Godparents

I wish I had fairy godparents
To cast wishes for anything I wanted,
I'd wish for one thousand wishes
I'd wish for chocolate
I'd wish for a nice babysitter
I'd wish for a sweet shop
I'd wish that I could mind-read
I'd wish for sun
I'd wish for fun
I'd wish for no school
I'd wish for it to be my birthday every day
I'd wish for this poem to end.

Stephanie Caisley (8)
Westville House School

Rugby

I like rugby, it is great
The best part is making a break
I like the ball
Its twist, its shape.

If I get the ball I fly for a try
If the enemy gets it I don't tackle high,
I like getting muddy
My clothes get all grubby.

A relaxing ice bath after the game
When I get in, I feel no pain,
I like tackling, it is the best
I don't go soft if they are a guest!

Sam Jeffrey (9)
Westville House School

The Monster In My TV

There's a monster in my TV
But Mum doesn't believe me.

Every time I sit down on the sofa
A great big hand comes and knocks me over.

The dog gets really scared
When the TV gets him unaware.

At night he snores
And shuts all the doors
So that we can't hear
When he is near.

Alasdair Kerr (9)
Westville House School

Seasons

Spring is when we see all the flowers,
The snowdrops and the daffodils.
All the lambs come out to play,
They twist and turn in all the fern.

Summer is a time to go on holiday,
And to have a water fight with our friends.
All the time you can play,
And a time for sheep to stray.

Autumn is a time to play in the leaves,
All the animals go cold so they start to shiver.
All the children stay inside,
It's to cold to go outside.

Winter is the time for snow,
Snowball fights start to go.
Christmas is in winter,
So everybody be jolly!

Ella McDowell (9)
Westville House School

There's A Ghost In My Garden

There's a ghost in my garden
I can't dream for it to be *dead!*

It even comes on holiday with
Us just because my mum said

I tell the ghost to go away
But he comes back and tries to play.

Well he's okay
I just want him to go away!

Hannah McGurk (9)
Westville House School

Winter

Winter is fun it can snow if you want
You can build a snowman made out of slushy snow
With a pipe and a carrot which is juicy
With a coloured scarf round its neck
With a black hat on his head
It would be good to play
In the snow
And you can sit by the fire
And drink hot chocolate
Plus you can melt marshmallows
It's good in winter because
You can do whatever you want to do.

Ellie Peden (8)
Westville House School

Summer

I like to lay on the beach all day
Sometimes I go fishing at the bay.

The sun is in the sky
I dream that I can fly.

I think the beach is hot
But in winter the beach is not!

I have lots of fun
I get my daily bun.

At the end of the day we have to go
I say to my mum, 'No, no!'

Jamie Moss (9)
Westville House School

Seasons

Spring is fresh,
The year has begun,
Lambs come out,
People having fun.

Summer is hot,
Go on holiday,
Not a cloud you could spot,
Just have fun and play.

Autumn means it's time now,
For leaves to fall and go away.
Farmers start to plough,
Conkers fall for kids to play.

Winter's cold,
Icy and white,
Balls of snow fall,
That are big and bold.

Elizabeth Roulston (9)
Westville House School

My Cruise

I go cruising in the sun
I lie down and have some fun
We go to lots of exciting places
Like Venice and Athens and Egypt.

There are lots of ships like
Aurora and Oceania and Arcadia
I go walking round the ship
And then I go back inside
So I recorded it.

Patrick Pointon (9)
Westville House School

There's A Monster In My Washing Machine

There's a monster in my washing machine
And it's eating all the clothes.

We need to wash my underpants
Now they've gone with the other clothes.

When we were washing all the clothes
The monster came out and swallowed me whole.

In the end I was too big
He burped, I fell out of it!

Dominic Zywicki (8)
Westville House School

Winter Poem

Winter is fun
We have loads of buns.

Snow is cold
Sledging is bold.

Robins sing loud and clear
While my dad drinks lots of beer.

Winter days are lots of fun
For everyone!

Claudia Pye (8)
Westville House School

The Snow

The snow is cold
And it is bold.
You will see
Snowflakes fold.

When I shiver
I see something quiver.
Snow is white
You might even get frostbite.

When you go inside next to the fire
There is always a little red choir.
When I have a snowball fight
We will stay and play all night.

When I make snowmen
The wind will blow them.

Jake Vaughan (8)
Westville House School

Imagine If I Was A Soldier

Imagine if I was a soldier,
Always getting hurt.

Imagine if I was a soldier,
Always killing people.

Imagine if I was a soldier,
Never seeing my family.

Imagine if I was a soldier,
Never seeing my mates.

Imagine if I wasn't a soldier,
I don't want to be a soldier.

Alexander Woodward (9)
Westville House School